THE SWAN EFFECT

Thriving with Impostor Syndrome

in the Digital Age

THE SWAN EFFECT

Thriving with Impostor Syndrome in the Digital Age

Cindy,

Thanks for your support!
Wishing you all the happiness
and success! Hope you enjoy
this read !! :)

CAROLINE A. RITTER

Caroline A. Ritter

NEW DEGREE PRESS
COPYRIGHT © 2021 CAROLINE A. RITTER
All rights reserved.

THE SWAN EFFECT
Thriving with Impostor Syndrome in the Digital Age

ISBN   978-1-63676-961-5   *Paperback*
          978-1-63730-027-5   *Kindle Ebook*
          978-1-63730-129-6   *Ebook*

To my family and friends—

*Thank you for giving me your endless support
and the courage to share my own words.*

To my fellow swans—

Keep swimming. You're doing great.

How others see you is not important.

How you see yourself means everything.

—UNKNOWN

TABLE OF CONTENTS

ACKNOWLEDGMENTS

With a special thanks to—

John and Andrea Ritter, Lauren Ritter, Brian Scotti, Dave and Maritoni Ritter and family, Kevin J. Van Horn, Matthew Kulesza, Zachary Kelly, Tyler Bridge, Justin Potisit, Myra Din, Nick Greco, Jake Shelton, Holly M. Ritter, Jimmy Franks, Montserrat Palacios, Carmen Rurak, Carissa Koetitz, Jean Ritter, Conor Fitzgerald, Kristina Alexander, Liam Carney, Kimberly Myles, Shambrekia Wise, Rashi Sahai, Cindy Celine Buffart, Taylor Fitzgerald, JP Burns, Melissa Young, Brianna Gardner, Jonathan Roach, Greg Leffert, Danielle Fitzpatrick, Jason Geytenbeek, Nicole Fabian, David Simon, Luis Cueva Gutiérrez, Dan Miltner, Scott Buckel, Ikram Saunders, Morgan Vazquez, Alex Senchak, Caroline Ritter, Michael Ippolito, Lauren Clemence, Phil H., Keith Karol, Andrew Jones, Brendan Cafferky, Mary Mecca, Victoria Ma, Billy Dombroski, Wendy Ritter, Meghan Desai, Phil Lehman, Kushali Marwaha, Thomas Tsang, Lily Applefield, Beau Warrington, Melissa D, Eric Koester, Sarah Phippen, Trevor Tezel, Ian Cruz, Drake Leonard, Varun G Hegde, Queena J Wang, Kelsey Navin, John H Walsh, Thomas Kingston, Celeste Groover, Thomas Damren, Kolby Keo, Andrew Gordineer, Kris Bolom, and Megan Roark.

INTRODUCTION
Success on the Surface:
Making *The Swan Effect*

———

"I've never had a job that I was qualified for."

To be honest, that wasn't exactly what I expected to hear from an established healthcare consultant in his early thirties who had recently considered starting his own practice.

I had directly asked him if he had ever felt like an impostor or a fraud before—like he was in way over his head just waiting for the day someone else would realize that too. His response was surprising to me. I thought this feeling was reserved for recent grads, career newbies, and people who were still trying to figure out exactly how to do this "adulting" thing five to seven days per week. This brief conversation began a series of enlightening discussions that changed the way I perceived the corporate ecosystem and the people in it.

* * *

Have you ever thought to yourself, *How did I even get here?* when you were stepping into a new office on your first day of work, or even a year or two later sitting at the same desk completely overwhelmed by a new assignment? It is that nagging feeling of not being "qualified." You get the new job or the promotion at work and suddenly question whether the hiring manager made a mistake and if you are even the right candidate for the job. You might be too nervous to speak up in a meeting and offer up a new idea because you feel you are still too young or inexperienced to provide a new insight. You get into graduate school and think the person who reviewed your application was feeling generous on the day they saw your file and didn't accept you because of your academic record or personal achievements.

If any of these situations sound familiar to you, you probably have experienced impostor syndrome—the feeling that your success was a result of luck or good timing rather than your own capabilities. This is usually coupled with the subsequent fear that someday other people will realize you are "unqualified" too, even though objectively you are successful.[1] If you have experienced this, you're certainly not alone in these feelings. Approximately 70 percent of people will experience impostor syndrome at least once in their lifetime.[2]

For me it happened shortly after I turned twenty-five. (Though admittedly at the time I had never heard of impostor syndrome before.) Pinpointing the exact moment when I started experiencing impostor syndrome is difficult, but I imagine these

---

1   John Gravois, "You're not fooling anyone," *The Chronicle of Higher Education,* November 9, 2007.

2   Jaruwan Sakulku and James Alexander, "The Impostor Phenomenon," *International Journal of Behavior Science* 6, no. 1 (2011): 73-92.

types of thoughts probably originated on the DC Metro while I was looking out of a smudged window and listening to my morning playlist as cars raced by on I-66. Surrounded by others headed into work who were staring down at their phones or trying to catch a few minutes of sleep, it was undoubtedly the perfect setting for some pre-work day contemplation. Trying to determine how I got to this exact place in my life—precisely on a 7:30 a.m. Silver Line train heading toward the towering office buildings of Tysons Corner, Virginia—was like trying to remember the plot line of a movie I had fast-forwarded through unknowingly. It was as if I had blinked too long at the age of eighteen and suddenly opened my eyes when I was a few years out of college with a job that on many days seemed way above my skillset. I had gone through the final exams and the campus interviews, but it still felt like I had fallen into my career path by chance rather than by my own capabilities.

Some may call this type of personal contemplation the beginning of a quarter-life crisis. In a survey conducted by LinkedIn of more than six thousand people in the United States, United Kingdom, India, and Australia, nearly 75 percent of people age twenty-five to thirty-three revealed that they've had or are currently going through their own quarter-life crisis, with career being the top cause of anxiety.[3] My "crisis" wasn't necessarily triggered by career discontent (though the hours in consulting can be less than ideal), but rather by the notion of not being able to rationalize to myself how I even got to that career in the first place. It was ironic that these feelings seemed to drop in at the moment when I thought I would have been hitting my stride. With almost three years of

3   Blair Heitmann, "Encountering a Quarter-life Crisis? You're Not Alone," *LinkedIn Online Blog,* November 15, 2017.

experience working at the same company, I thought I should have felt more settled or at least more comfortable with my routine and with myself. But then, more than ever, I found myself to be completely confused about where my career or even where my life was headed. I thought I would be confident enough to start seeking new job opportunities, but I started to question whether the bullet points on my resume were an accurate representation of my experience, or if I had somehow over-exaggerated my own abilities along the way. Weeks began to blur into months, and I thought I should start blocking off my calendar from 3:00 to 3:15 p.m. for my own daily existential crisis. Instead of grabbing a mid-afternoon coffee, I found myself staring at my computer screen and asking myself questions like, "What am I actually good at?" These types of questions obviously weren't going to be solved before I logged off for the day, so I shifted my focus back to client work.

Feeling like an "impostor" was exhausting. Finding the energy to get out of bed in the morning and to go to work was quite the struggle. I would make the trek home from my client site at the end of each day, take off my heels, and feel completely drained but slightly more at ease because I didn't have to fake a smile or give some canned response about how nice my weekend was. I felt like a fraud. The confident, put-together person who curled her hair almost every day for work seemed like an inauthentic version of myself. The perpetually exhausted twenty-five year old eating cereal for dinner while watching British baking competitions felt more like the "real" Caroline. I didn't want to show the world this version of myself and all of the paddling that I was doing underwater, so I became a true professional at social distancing before it was required and would cancel plans and strategically avoid human interaction outside of work. I didn't want anyone to see the "in progress" aspects of myself during this messy yet transformative period of personal growth. However, I worked hard to maintain an image in-person and online by filling up my Instagram with pictures of my new golden retriever puppy, Saturday brunches in DC, and networking galas. On the outside, it appeared I was flourishing and having the best year of my life. On the inside, I was continuing to struggle with the feeling that I was consistently not portraying an honest version of myself both virtually and in reality.

Fast forward a couple of weeks when I was sitting at the kitchen counter in my parent's house in New Jersey talking with my mom while she heated some water for tea, my newfound quarter-life crisis remedy. As I slowly stirred a pack of sugar into my steaming mug of jasmine green tea, I talked to her about my internal authenticity struggles and about how I felt like the past year of my life had been a "shit show," for lack of a better term. Standing up to place the now empty glass mugs in the sink, she briefly looked into the backyard and paused. When she turned around to speak, I could tell by the face she was making that she was probably about to say something enlightening or thought-provoking, at the very least. (I had seen a similar face many times before.) She reminded me of something a high school English teacher had once said about me during a parent-teacher conference. He said that I was like a swan—fully calm, composed, and graceful on the surface all the while paddling like hell under the water to get all my work done. I started to laugh as I began to remember the remark clearly. I hadn't thought about that comment in years. Granted, at that point in my life, my biggest concerns were final exams and finding a date to prom who was taller than me, but I think the underlying metaphor is very much still applicable in describing how we think about how others perceive us and how we perceive ourselves—the very basis of impostor syndrome.

The truth is that no one really knows what is beneath the surface for another person, except for maybe their closest friends and family. Any existing feelings of fraud and phoniness are deeply submerged beneath the polished version of a person, the composed swan, gliding effortlessly across the water. Those who are truly experiencing impostor syndrome never show it. This "swan effect" fascinated me; the idea that some people feel they are quickly swimming just to keep up with the fast-moving current when the world has a completely different view of them. The world only sees the objectively successful person on the surface. I wanted to dive deeper into this notion and how it has particularly impacted other millennials who, unlike generations before, have had to keep up an image both in-person and online. The rise of the Digital Age and social media have forever changed concepts of personal identity and self-growth because of the inherent pressure to portray a filtered and fulfilling life across their online profiles. As a society we are often scared to show we are a work-in-progress and only choose to display the most beautiful, carefully curated versions of ourselves, because that's what seems to get more "likes." However, a disconnect between the life we post and the life we live can cause us to question our own authenticity.

I first stumbled across the term "impostor syndrome" when I was in the weeds of psychological journals that explored notions of identity, authenticity, and social media. Truthfully, when I began writing this book, I solely wanted to explore other people's experiences feeling like an impostor in the age of Facebook, Instagram, and LinkedIn. I was interested in knowing how they had coped with their own feelings of inauthenticity and what propelled them to keep swimming in hopes that I could learn how to face my own impostor syndrome and then perhaps share what I learned with others in similar situations. I went out and asked difficult questions. I asked friends, acquaintances, and even strangers from a variety of backgrounds if they had ever felt like a fraud before in some aspect of their lives and, in turn, if they had ever feared that someone would figure out they were a fraud. I was not expecting that my exploration into personal accounts of impostor syndrome would completely shift my perspective. I was able to see that this "syndrome" is not really a syndrome at all, as the word largely denotes something undesirable or negative. As a matter of fact, there were actually key benefits to being a so-called "impostor." The people who had experienced similar feelings of being "unqualified" shared certain key attributes, inherent to having impostor syndrome, that equipped them to be successful. Whether they had realized it or not, they had been able to leverage their own impostor syndrome to create an *impostor advantage* for themselves.

The term "*impostor advantage*" may seem like an odd combination of words, because how can there be an advantage to being an impostor? This expression refers to the positive edge, or rather the benefits, which can be created from having impostor syndrome and feeling like a fraud. Though someone may have not felt qualified for the job or situation at hand, they have the personal qualifications to be successful through being an "impostor." For example, people who believe their success is based on luck or good timing rather than their own capabilities are likely to be more humble, more appreciative, and have more gratitude toward opportunities. In other words, if you believe you are lucky to be where you are, that you were the exception that slipped through the cracks to get the job or to get into the selective program, you are more likely to be grateful about having such an opportunity and more likely to make the most out of it. Aside from humility, this book explains the key characteristics of impostors that enable their individual successes and why these characteristics are so important in the Digital Age.

So, *The Swan Effect* became less about impostor syndrome itself and more about shifting the narrative. I have read many articles that explained *how* individuals with impostor syndrome tend to be some of the most successful individuals, even if they don't immediately believe that themselves. However, not any of these articles clearly explained *why* individuals with impostor syndrome were actually successful. They instead focused on how to combat the syndrome, particularly in the workplace. Instead of trying to propose alternative methods to "cure" the inner questioning voice, I wanted to explore impostor syndrome as a tipping point for success and not a consequence of it. There are plenty of discussions on people who have "made it" and then feel like impostors in their respective fields, but what about the people who already feel like impostors who are just starting out in or shifting their careers? I wrote *The Swan Effect* to uncover why impostors are so successful in the first place and to share why embracing impostor syndrome is so important.

I admitted that I have questioned my own qualifications at work, but deciding to write a book was one of the most challenging experiences with impostor syndrome I have ever faced. There is something very ironic about writing a book *about* impostor syndrome when you are writing the book *with* impostor syndrome. Great hands-on research, I suppose? I was terrified to even tell anyone about my author journey because I didn't feel qualified to write *this* book or even *a* book in the first place. What made me fit to write over a hundred pages on such a topic? Why would anyone want to read or hear what I have to say about impostor syndrome in the Digital Age if I am not a psychologist, researcher, or expert on the characteristics of the "workforce of the future"? I realized that fixating on these questions would not inspire me to write or finish the book. I was too caught up in whether I was "qualified" to be doing what I was doing and how other people would perceive my qualifications. The fear of not being capable enough was holding me back from seeing what I actually could accomplish. I kept minimizing the value of my message, and I struggled to put words on paper for months, until I started shifting my thought patterns. I began to slowly accept that my own messages *did* matter because they were shaped by my own thoughts and experiences. I have a unique perspective to offer, and being vulnerable enough to share that perspective is important. I began to worry less about *who* would want to read my book and more about *why* I was writing—the key thoughts that I wanted to share in hopes of potentially helping someone else who may currently be experiencing impostor syndrome. There is a common misconception when writing a book that you must be an established authority on the topic; however, this book is the result of my own personal learning process with impostor syndrome. The pages are filled with over a year's worth of researching, reading, interviewing, listening, and self-reflection.

I hope this book will provide a new perspective for those who believe they are struggling with feeling like an "impostor" as they go through phases of personal and professional growth. This book is for anyone who has asked themselves at least once, "How did I even get here?" and "What am I actually good at?" and hasn't been able to find the answers just yet. Impostor syndrome isn't a very widely discussed topic due to the nature of it—people don't usually want to admit they feel like frauds—so I am writing to normalize these feelings so that others may be able to relate their own personal experiences. For those who haven't identified with it yet, I hope this book will prepare them to acknowledge and accept future experiences.

Additionally, I hope this book will encourage individuals in management and leadership positions to consider how impostor syndrome may affect individuals on their own teams so they can create an inclusive working environment that supports success. By defining and unpacking terms such as "qualification" and "accomplishment," I hope to provide a new view on recognizing qualifications and accomplishments in today's environment where self-expectations are set very high and showcasing achievements online is commonplace. The next one-hundred-odd pages may not change your life, but I hope it may start to change your perspective on impostor syndrome and authenticity in the workplace.

The Swan Effect is written in three sections. The first section explores the history of the term "impostor syndrome" and its prevalence in the Digital Age, the second section defines the components or personal characteristics of the *impostor advantage*, and the final section explains why leveraging the *impostor advantage* and embracing impostor syndrome can be the beginning of your own success story.

PART I

Impostor Syndrome in the Digital Age

CHAPTER 1

The History of "Fake It 'til You Make It"

———

"Fake it 'til you make it" is the cliché advice often given to others facing stressful moments in their career, such as important client presentations or "dream job" interviews. If you are able to fake confidence in these high-stakes situations, you will be successful, according to this phrase. They may seem like harmless words of wisdom, until you consider an alternative meaning: showing confidence without feeling 100 percent confident on the inside is "fake."

Does forged confidence make someone inauthentic in the workplace? Is it difficult to accept success that is achieved when you are deceiving other people into thinking you are confident? If impostor syndrome had a catch phrase, it would definitely be "fake it 'til you make it."

* * *

Impostor syndrome, also known as the impostor phenomenon, impostorism, fraud syndrome, or the impostor experience, was first defined in the late 1970s. In the same year that *Grease* hit drive-in movie theaters, Dr. Pauline Clance and Dr. Suzanne Imes conducted a study on 150 women who had received recognition in their respective fields and had high levels of achievement evidenced by academic degrees and standardized test scores. Despite their apparent accomplishments, these women could not acknowledge their own successes, which they reasoned were a result of good luck, chance, and the opportune timing of events. They believed the accolades they received from colleagues were an exaggeration of their actual capabilities and knowledge. These feelings of being a "fraud" were combined with symptoms of depression, anxiety, and noticeably low levels of self-confidence.[4]

Impostorism is the feeling that you don't deserve your own success because it was a result of good timing and "being in the right place at the right time" rather than personal abilities. This is coupled with the fear that one day your true identity and "fraudulent success" will be exposed to others, who will then not like the real version of yourself. The research done by Dr. Clance and Dr. Imes led to further studies that revealed this phenomenon affects more than just successful women.[5] It impacts people from all walks of life at all stages of life as they question their own personal, academic, or professional achievements. As I already noted, the majority of people will experience impostor phenomenon at least once.

Impostor syndrome can be explained by the distinction between feelings and facts. That you have achieved X, Y, and

---

4   Pauline R. Clance and Suzanne Imes, "The Impostor Phenomenon in High Achieving Women: Dynamics and Therapeutic Intervention," *Psychotherapy: Theory, Research & Practice 15*, no. 3 (1978): 241–247.

5   Ibid.

Z is a fact. You even have evidence of these achievements, such as the very expensive piece of paper you got when you graduated from college or the bi-weekly pay stub you receive from the job you thought was way above your head. However, it is a feeling, not a fact, when you think or believe your achievements were not based on your own capabilities and were instead just a result of good timing or good luck. The admissions officers looking at your application or the hiring manager at the firm where you are interviewing only see the facts, the tangible accomplishments, on your CV or resume, and they do not see that you achieved these successes based on luck or faking it until you made it. As such, impostor syndrome runs contrary to the actual facts.

To further explain what causes people to feel this way, Dr. Clance defined the "impostor cycle," which typically begins with some sort of new academic or work-related event that triggers anxiety in an individual about their ability to successfully complete the task at hand. This phenomenon is more likely to occur with a new accomplishment or milestone when the feelings of fraud creep in along with the uncertainty. Even if the individual receives positive feedback regularly about what they've done when they have completed a task or achieved a milestone, they attribute their success to over-preparation or luck and not their own intellectual capabilities. According to this mindset, a presentation went well because of all of the last-minute preparation the night before or a stroke of luck in the moment of "just winging it." The impostor phenomenon is marked by several other personal characteristics, including the need to feel special, perfectionism, fear of failure, denial of positive feedback, and even the fear of success because it may lead to higher expectations from others. Prolonged feelings of phoniness can have negative psychological impacts. A key element of impostorism is concealing feelings of unworthiness from others, so these feelings may be internalized and persistently draining. Feeling that you are pretending to be confident every day is undeniably exhausting.[6]

Sometimes feelings of insecurity and self-doubt may actually inspire someone to work harder due to the fear of being "exposed as a phony"; however, that may actually lead to increasing feelings of fraud syndrome with the added examples of success and recognition. Increasing self-doubt can be dangerous not only because of the psychological impacts of anxiety and depression, but also for the rising potential for a "self-fulfilling prophecy" to occur. In terms of the impostor phenomenon, the self-fulfilling prophecy would mean that repeated failure to acknowledge personal achievements and to be confident in personal capabilities may ultimately hinder success as individuals shy away from new opportunities and experiences for fear of failure or fear of exposure of what they believe to be their own incompetence. Fear of inadequacy becomes the reason for reaching an impasse in life. If someone feels like they earned their current job by luck rather than merit, they may not be likely to ask for a promotion or to apply to a different job that may be more advanced, thus limiting their own potential growth. Without the opportunities to receive a reward or an advancement, "success" becomes less attainable.[7] To prevent this from happening, it's important to shift the narrative—your own narrative—to

---

6   Jaruwan Sakulku and James Alexander, "The Impostor Phenomenon," *International Journal of Behavior Science* 6, no. 1 (2011): 73-92.

7   Cari Rom, "Impostor Syndrome Can Be a Self-Fulfilling Prophecy," *The Cut*, November 16, 2016.

replace impostor syndrome thoughts with *impostor advantage* thoughts and to remove self-limiting thought patterns.

The impostor phenomenon impacts nearly everyone, no matter how "successful" they may seem to be on the outside. Maya Angelou, a celebrated American poet and civil rights activist, once said, "I have written eleven books, but each time I think, uh oh, they're going to find out now. I've run a game on everybody, and they're going to find me out." Sheryl Sandberg, once named on *Time 100*'s most influential people in the world list and the current chief operating officer of Facebook, has said, "There are still days when I wake up feeling like a fraud, not sure I should be where I am." In an interview with *The New York Times*, the former CEO of Starbucks, Howard Schultz, revealed his own inner questioning voice when he said, "Very few people, whether you've been in that job before or not, get into the seat and believe today that they are now qualified to be the CEO. They're not going to tell you that, but it's true." Objectively speaking I think we can agree that these are all people who have achieved great things in their respective lifetimes, yet they still feel as though one day they will be "figured out" and their success will be diminished. That no one is completely immune from these feelings of insecurity is evident. To some extent, everyone has a fear that what they have achieved has only been a case of good timing, and the foundation to their success is really a house of cards that could easily be blown over by reality. The irony of the imposter phenomenon is that the success does not improve the situation and the more that someone accomplishes, the more likely they are to feel like a fraud. This is due not to a lack of success but rather the lack of ability to *internalize* success.[8]

---

8   Rose Leadem, "12 Leaders, Entrepreneurs and Celebrities Who Have Struggled With Imposter Syndrome," *Entrepreneur,* November 8, 2017.

It's not surprising that the impostor phenomenon is not a very widely discussed topic and not something people like to talk about from their own perspective often, as it could potentially expose the "fraud" or "phoniness" they may feel like they are living. However, most of the people who I interviewed had at least heard of impostor syndrome before, whether or not they admitted experiencing it themselves. That being said, impostor syndrome can ironically be difficult to self-diagnose. Some people may be able to accept that others can experience it but may feel like they are actually real impostors with no real qualifications just faking their way along in life.

With so many major milestones and new life experiences that occur between the ages of twenty to thirty, it is understandable why this decade can be full of uncertainty and self-doubt — making it extremely vulnerable to the impostor phenomenon. During this period, people typically graduate from college, begin their careers, decide to go back to graduate school, get into serious relationships or get married, and even start families. With each new milestone, it is reasonable to reflect back on everything that led up to a life-defining moment, but sometimes that reflection can be filled with overwhelming feelings of unworthiness and questions such as, Do I really deserve this job? Am I smart enough to be getting this degree? and Does this person like me for who I really am? I'm sure some people out there start a new job and say, "Wow, I am so prepared for this. I have all the right qualifications, and I deserve to be here." (And those people probably don't need to read this book.) However, for the rest of us, new beginnings bring new anxieties.

In order to better understand how impostor syndrome affects Generation Y in the Digital Age outside of my own personal experiences, I created a survey to ask a group of millennials ten relatively simple questions about their experiences with social media, personal identity, their greatest achievements, and impostor syndrome. In this survey, I left the name field optional as those who grapple with impostor syndrome may feel uncomfortable admitting to other people that they feel or have felt like an impostor at some point in their lives. (By creating anonymity, I hoped that people would feel more comfortable in sharing their true experiences.) The survey was distributed to people from a variety of different backgrounds and career paths with respondent ages ranging from twenty-one to thirty-five.

The respondents represented a large breadth of fields, including science, law, banking and finance, marketing and advertising, and human resources. When asked if they had ever heard of impostor syndrome before and if so, in what context, over 80 percent of respondents had heard of impostor syndrome in either a professional or academic setting described as a feeling of not belonging. From an outside perspective, all of the people who participated in the survey seemed to be living successful lives; however, over 85 percent of survey respondents indicated they felt they achieved based on luck and good timing rather than completely by their own capabilities. More than one individual attributed receiving a job because they knew the right person who was able to make a connection for them. Job placement was also attributed to hiring managers needing a quick replacement despite being under-qualified. College and law school acceptances were attributed to "happy accidents," letters of recommendation from influential people, and pure luck. Only a few people felt that both luck and merit were crucial components to their achievements.

I asked survey takers if they had ever felt like they were "faking it until they make it" and if so, to explain the context of the situation.

The majority of people felt like they were "faking it" in a professional sense, and this how they responded:

"As a young lawyer, we are often given assignments without enough instruction [and it's] where I do my best without knowing if it's the right way to do things."

—LAWYER, TWENTY-FIVE

"Yes, some project tasks require me to Google answers, and I wonder if peers already know."

—PROJECT MANAGER, THIRTY-FIVE

"With work I always apply for a role that's slightly above the level where I think I am, and when I get in I just fake it (a.k.a. spend a lot of time learning things to get up to speed) until I figure out how to do it."

—CUSTOMER INSIGHTS SENIOR MANAGER, TWENTY-NINE

"When I started at my firm I felt out of place. I started with several individuals who achieved what I thought was more than me, and/or attended more prestigious colleges. It made me feel like I had something to prove and that I had to work harder."

—BUSINESS CONSULTANT, TWENTY-SIX

And my personal favorite:

"There have been instances where a client has looked to me for guidance or an opinion, and I've felt like two kids in a trench coat masquerading as the authority in the room."

—LAWYER, THIRTY

I had my first lesson on "fake it 'til you make it" long before I entered the workforce. When I was about six years old my parents decided it was a good time to sign up my older sister and me for Tang Soo Do karate. Though I could barely tie my Reebok sneakers on my own, I was learning how to do knuckle push-ups on a hardwood floor, how to count to ten in Korean, and how to let out intimidating yells when I kicked a punching bag. However, the most important lessons I learned in karate actually had nothing to do with punching or kicking.

Five years after I started, I was preparing to test for my black belt. I was practicing movements in the mirror and getting frustrated every time I forgot a step or did something wrong. I was nervous that I was going to mess up during the actual evaluation and embarrass myself in front of the instructors and other students. Seeing my frustration, the owner of the karate studio walked over to me and in an upbeat tone said, "Fake it 'til you make it, girl." It took a few minutes for my twelve-year-old brain to understand what he was implying. He was encouraging me to act like I was confident on the studio floor when I was doing a sequence of punches and kicks, even if I didn't really feel that way at the time, and eventually I would be confident going through the motions. I mean, the logic was flawless, right? I have often thought about this piece of advice before big presentations, interviews, and any other seemingly nerve-rattling life event. If I just acted confident in what I was doing, everything would turn out just fine. As I got older, I realized that was far too simplistic. There would always be the next assignment, the next presentation, or the next interview in the future to be concerned about. No one ever specified when the "faking it" would end and when (or if) the authentic confidence would begin.

Well, my twenty-six-year-old brain has a different perspective on what "fake it 'til you make it" actually means.

This phrase creates and reinforces impostor syndrome. Let's say you are preparing for an interview for your dream job. You're nervous about how you will compare to the other candidates and if you will be able to seamlessly answer the questions the hiring manager asks you. Someone gives you the advice to "fake it 'til you make it," and you have this thought in the back of your mind as you are walking into the interview. You sit down with the interviewer, articulately speak about your relevant experience and why you are a good fit for the position, and answer all of their questions confidently without having to think twice. A week later you receive a call from the recruiter congratulating you for getting the job, and you think to yourself, *Wow, I made it—surprisingly!* However, this undermines your own capabilities. "Faking it" implies having to pretend or put on a show to achieve something when, in actuality, if you were able to confidently respond to the interviewer, then you already had that confidence before the interview even started.

No, you didn't fool the interviewer. "Faking it" really was just bringing out something that you didn't know you already had. Thinking in terms of "faking" makes the confidence or the experience that you portrayed seem like something forged or something that doesn't truly belong to you. It may make your own success seem to be built on false foundations as well. This example can be applied to more than just job interviews, but it shows the self-limiting power of words. Impostor syndrome originates in these types of phrases and thought patterns around inauthenticity. Creating the *impostor advantage* involves altering thought patterns to understand the importance of both authentic confidence as well as authentic uncertainty.

Impostor syndrome in the Digital Age is complex. It is an intersection point of multiple areas of importance (if not challenge) for millennials. These areas include technology, social media comparison culture, career, mental health, and notions of success. Impostor syndrome is not a new psychological concept, but it is more challenging to address than ever before.

CHAPTER 2

The World Is Your Oyster Paradox:

Technology and Impostor Syndrome

———

How many times in your life has someone told you that "you can do anything you set your mind to," or some variation of the phrase?

This mentality combined with the ability to explore endless opportunities has created a paradox in the Digital Age. The "world is your oyster" paradox explains how technology and the "you can do anything you want to" culture has encouraged impostor syndrome.

* * *

Impostor syndrome has been inevitably changed, if not worsened, by technology and the high visibility, social media-obsessed, success-focused culture it has created.

The Digital Age has arguably exacerbated feelings of "not being qualified" for millennials (and boomers). With technology advancing at a rapid pace and constant innovation, the potential for having to learn something new and adapt quickly in the workforce is exponentially increasing, which can lead to feelings of unpreparedness or uncertainty. Outside of the office, the significance of social media and the underlying forces of social comparison online have amplified the pressure to achieve and also the pressure to display achievements. This raises the question as to whether the era of social platforms has made the impostor phenomenon even more likely to occur.

Every single aspect of life, including how we shop, how we work, and how we form relationships, has been impacted for better or for worse by technology. The breadth of information available online presents endless opportunities yet overwhelming options. The influx of workout tips from Instagram influencers, podcasts on how to start a business from scratch, and meditation lifestyle apps has no doubt compelled a growth-oriented, self-improvement mindset for many. However, this mindset of constantly needing to improve upon oneself can be coupled with unrealistic expectations and feelings of failure for simply not being able to do it all. We live in a world where people can easily build income online by picking up their phone and connecting with others to sell products or services. However, we also now live in a world where the lines of work-life balance have been blurred because of the capability to work remotely and the expectations to be responsive even outside of normal working hours.

A 2018 study by Nielsen, a market-research group, revealed that on average, American adults spend more than eleven hours per day in front of screens, which was up over two hours from a similar study conducted four years before.[9] Technology has caused us to be powered on, plugged in, and constantly consuming information nearly every moment we are not sleeping. And if we are still awake, we might start to feel guilty about not being plugged in, not being productive, or not working toward our next big life-changing goal. If theoretically we can do anything we set our minds to, and there are so many opportunities available to us online, then that would mean the only thing stopping us from doing more or achieving more is ourselves, right? Being busy and having limited free time is glamorous because the "world is your oyster" mentality tells us the harder we work on something and the more time that we put into it, the more accomplishments we will see come from the time invested. In a perfect world, this would seem like a logical assumption—that the formula to success includes a variable for the number of hours put toward an activity. However, when we get to the end of an eight-hour or (more realistically) a twelve-hour work day and see that our daily to-do list barely decreased, it's easy to feel frustrated, defeated, and guilty for not doing or being enough. It's easy to blame our lack of productivity on ourselves and what we are lacking then to acknowledge what might have sidetracked the day or hindered progress. The "should haves" start rolling in as "I should have woken up earlier to start my work for the day" or "I should have approached that meeting or task differently."

Impostor syndrome sneaks in with these thoughts of not being productive; of not meeting the expectations that we set for ourselves; of not being "enough." The disappointment

---

9   Quentin Fottrell, "People Spend Most of Their Waking Hours Staring at Screens," *MarketWatch*, August 4, 2018.

that we have in ourselves is only outweighed by the fear of disappointing others and not meeting the expectations we believe they have set for us. It's a fear that we will appear as weak or not qualified when our "human-ness" is revealed and we aren't able to go above and beyond on the task at hand. I have struggled with these feelings myself while working in a fast-paced field in which I am consistently younger and comparably less-experienced than the clients who I am contracted to work with on a daily basis. I often worried they would perceive "less experience" as plain "inexperience," and that if I didn't accomplish every task thrown at me, then I simply wasn't qualified to be in the role I was given. I wasn't allowing myself to be human, to have limitations, or to set boundaries with myself or other people. I truly thought that if I wasn't doing everything that everyone asked of me, then I wasn't doing enough. My constant focus was on proving to other people that I was capable and confident, even if that meant sacrificing a lot of my own personal time and needs. I allowed work, and more specifically my performance at work, to become a large part of my post-college personal identity, an identity that technology has continually molded.

With the deep integration of technology in everyday life, it is not surprising that the Digital Age has even affected something as intricate as personal identity formation. The rise of social media platforms has caused identity and sense of self to largely be developed through an external rather than an internal process—the concept of focusing on portraying oneself versus creating oneself. When millennials born in the 1990s began entering the formative years of adolescence, they had the opportunity to use AOL screennames to create profiles on MySpace after its initial launch in 2003. The popularity of social media continued to rise as Facebook entered the picture only a few years later. Social media had become a powerful sociological force driven by advances in internet technology, the invention of the smart phone, and the basic human desire to form personal connections.[10] In this important phase for developing an independent sense of identity, the emergence of mirror selfies on Myspace and the introduction of the "like" feature on Facebook fostered an online environment driven by external validation and gratification. These social sites gave users the ability to create personalized online profiles displayed to the public, providing a platform to explore and construct identities. Social media platforms have the unique ability to allow us to quite literally edit the aesthetics of our personal brand and identity at any given time by deleting the posts, pictures, and people who no longer fit into the image of ourselves that we want to convey. Fearing a lack of response or even criticism, online identities were created to show only the best aspects of self. Those aspects that were not as "likeable" or still a work-in-progress were kept offline. However, by constantly being plugged in and focusing on the upkeep of an online image, there was inherently less focus on introspection and self-reflection, the key internal aspects of identity formation.

I asked impostor syndrome survey-takers if growing up during the rise of social media has impacted their personal identity at all. The responses included numerous examples of how social media has made individuals feel less confident in themselves because they began comparing themselves and their life accomplishments "to people that they shouldn't," including filtered images of celebrities, and being cautious about what they post because they didn't want it to ruin

---

10   "The Evolution of Social Media: How Did It Begin and Where Could It Go Next?" Maryville Online, Maryville University, March 3, 2021.

the image that they have created online. One person went as far as to say social media "hampers your ability to find your identity, as it gets you wrapped up in what other people think." Female respondents in particular felt that social media had impacted the way in which they saw "pretty" or "happy" as they compared themselves to women that they saw online and felt more insecure in their own posts. Besides comparing looks, survey takers also noted comparing their social lives to the other users they followed on social media, which in turn made them feel "boring," "less fortunate," or "behind" in relation to their peers.

Extreme social comparison is very much a symptom of the Digital Age and a burden for millennials and the generations that follow. The capability to see hundreds of people with the same age, same background, same interests, and/or even same career within minutes of scrolling makes comparison far too simple, whether consciously or subconsciously. If you're a female in her twenties, a search on Instagram may reveal Kylie Jenner who has a net worth of one billion dollars and flawless skin and Kayla Itsines who regularly displays her solid abs and at-home workouts. Though these profiles are mostly based on skillful branding rather than accurate representations of everyday life, it can be difficult to distinguish between the two. More than any other generation before, millennials are aware of the accomplishments of their peers and how they stack up against those accomplishments. The rise of Instagram influencers and carefully created online profiles has arguably created a very shallow environment of people showing only the best versions of themselves. The burden to create a perfect, polished profile and the inescapable disconnect from the imperfect, unpolished reality of everyday life can heighten feelings of perceived deception in the real world. Portraying an idealistic representation of yourself online promotes feelings of inauthenticity and self-doubt, as impostor syndrome extends beyond self-doubt around intelligence to also encompass popularity and attractiveness. In consequence, the person who edits their photos to cover their own blemishes with the hopes of receiving more likes becomes more embarrassed of their true self. They fear being seen naturally without makeup and without a filter because it could reveal the misalignment between virtual and real identity.

Personal identity is a dynamic combination of constancy and change. There are aspects of our identities that remain constant year after year and aspects that change as we go through the different stages of life since our personal identities are an evolving blend of our upbringing and our experiences. Think about the person who you were even just four years ago. How different is that person from the person you see in the mirror today? (And I'm not just talking about appearance.) During the major transition periods of life—middle school to high school, high school to college, college to post-college, one career field to another—opportunities are presented for personal redefinition. The identity that you held in the previous phase of your life can be remolded and reshaped in your hands and then reintroduced to the world. When you went off to college and no one knew your name or your high school reputation, you were able to choose what the 2.0 version of yourself would be like in this next stage. At least there was still some element of certainty in moving on from high school to college, as you still had the structure that came with your classes and extra-curricular activities. The post-college identity transition was perhaps something you didn't expect. Suddenly the structure was gone, and you were

CHAPTER 2:   ·   45

out on your own looking for the next step in your life. You jumped headfirst into grad school or your first career without looking back until one day you were on your morning commute two or three years post-grad and suddenly thinking, *How did I get here?*

Some have referred to this early period of deep questioning and uncertainty as a "quarter-life crisis," since you are still about twenty years out from the age that people start buying Corvette convertibles and getting Botox to cope with these deep feelings of uncertainty. You start thinking about where you are in terms of the big life milestones for your age group, such as getting married and buying your first home. Besides the regular afternoon existential crisis and general malaise, there are other signs and symptoms that you may be experiencing a quarter-life crisis:

- You have been out of college for a few years now, but you still don't really know what you want to be when you grow up.

- You feel sad looking at other people's lives play out over social media because you thought that you would have been in a different place in your life by now.

- You have slight feelings of dread when you have to attend an obligatory family event because you will have to answer the very generalized question "How are things?" around five to seven times.

Is this "crisis" a rite of passage faced by every generation, or is it a more of consequence of the increasingly digital world that we live in? Think about it for a minute. Previous generations were not accustomed to having their lives play out online. They were not constantly compelled (whether consciously or subconsciously) to compare their lives to other people as they scrolled down Instagram feeds and watched Snapchat stories. In an interview with *Business Insider*, clinical psychologist Alex Fowke spoke about the "intense pressure" millennials are experiencing "to get themselves onto the housing market, navigate the increasingly complex professional landscape, struggle to maintain relationships in addition to being commonly subjected to a distorted notion of life through social media." He added "key challenges faced by people aged from between eighteen and thirty-five can include identity confusion, internal conflict (failing to reach the expectations set for themselves) and uncertainty."[11] Arguably, more so than any generation before, millennials have experienced the realities of forming identity and transitioning to adulthood in the Digital Age.

Technology has made the identity formation process increasingly complex and increasingly prone to impostor syndrome, which has been felt most by the generation that has grown up during the rise of social networking—the millennials. Identity built online is constructed upon inherently fragile foundations—on high expectations, unobtainable perfection, the near-constant need for validation, and a lot of filtered photos. As millennials like myself move further into independence and into what reality looks like, it becomes evidently clear that those foundations are not sustainable and certainly not helpful toward reaching self-fulfillment or personal happiness. When adulthood finally hits with all of the delights of greater responsibility, paying bills, and remembering to feed yourself, a harsh reality starts to set in that choices have to be made, and editing life is not as simple as clicking the upload

11   Rosie Fitzmaurice, "This is the exact age when you're most likely to experience a quarter-life crisis—and how to deal with it if you do," *Insider*, November 5, 2017.

or delete buttons. Real life is complicated, messy, and can't always be tied up in a neat, polished package for the world to see, which can make our online personas seem phony or insincere. Internal struggles with authenticity and the fear of showing imperfection are symptoms of a digital environment that is based on how we appear to others.

As the Digital Age has significantly impacted how we create and mold our own personal identities, it has also impacted how we achieve, why we achieve, and how we share our achievements with other people.

In some ways, the Digital Age has made achievement and even success seem more accessible. Online learning, degrees, and certifications allow people to collect academic and professional accomplishments in a less traditional, but completely normalized, manner. Without having to relocate or commute to an academic institution to obtain a degree, learning has arguably become more obtainable and available. Additionally, people are able to start up new side hustles in seconds, selling products online through their own personal social media profiles. However, has this accessibility been a double-edged sword for Generation Y? A survey by the American Psychiatric Association in 2018 revealed that millennials are the overall most anxious generation in comparison to Baby Boomers and Generation Z, though Generation Z isn't too far behind.[12] A key reason that millennials have cited for their anxiety is feeling overwhelmed about making decisions—largely because of a multitude of options they have. In other words, the information overload online has

---

12 "Americans Say They Are More Anxious Than a Year Ago; Baby Boomers Report Greatest Increase in Anxiety," American Psychiatric Association, May 7, 2018.

presented so many choices for a career that millennials are nervous about making the wrong decisions.[13] The Digital Age has provided many more opportunities, but with those opportunities comes a fear of not doing or achieving enough.

In addition to the pressure to succeed, we now live in an age where we are compelled to also share our achievements—to put them on display for the world to see online, selectively, of course. This has become the new norm—to showcase the highlights of our lives for others to view, like, or comment on. This kind of sharing makes you think about how much society has changed its perspective and methodology for displaying and receiving positive information. Your grandparents probably didn't pay for a large space in the local newspaper when your mom and dad graduated from college and got their first job or a big promotion at work. Everything seems to have been lot more private back then—your achievements were known by those closest to you, your family, and the random strangers that your grandmother struck up conversation with at the grocery store. As millennials, we display our achievements and accomplishments across social networking platforms—our academic and professional achievements are highlighted on our LinkedIn pages, and happy, personal accomplishments are posted on our Facebook or Instagram accounts. People may have multiple reasons for sharing their successes online, whether it is to build up professional credentials for potential employers or recruiters to see, to keep far-away family and friends in the loop about exciting life events, or to simply get the ego-boost from receiving likes and comments.

---

13   Tess Brigham, "I've been a 'millennial therapist' for more than 5 years— and this is their number 1 complaint," *CNBC Make It: Science of Success*, July 2, 2019.

The reasons for sharing online are inherently biological. In a paper titled "Disclosing Information About the Self Is Intrinsically Rewarding," two neuroscientists from Harvard published research supporting that when people talk about their own experiences, a dopamine response is set off in their brain. In fact, studies on the brain activity of people discussing their own thoughts showed that a reward response was triggered, similar to the response triggered by receiving food or money. This research solidified that, as social creatures, there is a natural human tendency to want to share things about yourself.[14] Though bragging or boasting is largely frowned upon in everyday conversation (and will likely produce some questionable looks from people listening in), sharing achievements online is normal now, if not expected. When our friends get engaged or graduate from law school, we expect to see a post about it, or at least a picture to commemorate the event on Instagram. This raises the question if there is overall more pressure to post about achievements because of how important social media has become in our lives, and with that pressure to post, if there is overall more pressure to have achievements in the first place. Whether we consciously think about it or not, social networking sites perpetuate social comparison. In scrolling down feeds, we can easily see all of the recent achievements of our friends and followers. This hyper-awareness of the milestones that other people are achieving may leave us thinking about how we measure up and if we are achieving enough ourselves.

As mentioned earlier in this chapter, technology has not only encouraged impostor syndrome online in how we compare

14   Diana Tamir and Jason Mitchell, "Disclosing Information about the Self Is Intrinsically Rewarding", *PNAS*, National Academy of Sciences, May 2, 2012.

ourselves to others, but also at work as we compare our own knowledge and skillsets to the roles and projects we are given. Innovation has increased the probability that someone will encounter a system or process they have never seen before and will have to adapt to new ways of working. This unfamiliarity may cause someone to question if they are prepared at all. The Digital Age has been characterized by rapid change and technological advancements that impact nearly every aspect of our lives, including how and what we do for work. Companies have embraced cutting-edge innovation, such as automation and artificial intelligence, which have transformed entire organizations and simultaneously created and eliminated roles. As many companies change to more agile business models, employees will fulfill certain functions based on the current needs and priorities of the company, which requires a high level of flexibility and comfortableness, or at least a familiarity, with being uncomfortable.[15]

The next chapter of this book will begin to explain why impostor syndrome, the inner questioning voice, and the ability to excel in situations outside of your comfort zone are invaluable in the Digital Age. Being the type of person who wonders if they are doing enough, who is cognizant of their own abilities and limitations, and who continues to push forward anyway has key advantages. While technology has encouraged the impostor phenomenon, it has also created working environments that require aspects embedded within impostor syndrome. Personal characteristics inherent to the self-proclaimed impostors, frauds, and phonies prepare them for continued success.

---

15   Jacques Bughin et al., "Rethinking Work in the Digital Age," *McKinsey Quarterly,* October 24, 2016.

CHAPTER 3

Defining the *Impostor Advantage*

———

The term "impostor" by itself usually refers to someone who is a fraud. However, "impostor" as used in this book to refer to someone with impostor syndrome is more aptly described with the following definition.

Impostor /im'paster/

(n.) Someone who believes that their own successes are due to luck or good timing but continues to achieve amazing things despite their insecurities.

see also: brave, limit-pusher, risk-taker, innovator, entrepreneur

* * *

Outwardly impostor syndrome sounds like something you do not want to have. The word "impostor" has a negative connotation—a fraud, a phony, or a person pretending to be someone else to deceive others. Then "syndrome" is normally used to describe a group of symptoms or signs that indicate a problem. Put them together and these words refer to a person who believes they are unqualified or unfit for the success they have achieved. Though in the context of impostor syndrome, the "impostor" is not truly deceiving anyone else, yet the combination of words still seems to carry a certain stigma and signify a personal problem to be fixed. Admitting to the personal uncertainty or lack of confidence associated with impostorism is difficult. However, the "impostor" is someone who continues to push through their own insecurities and self-doubt to achieve things they didn't originally believe they could. Impostor syndrome is not a hindrance to success. In fact, it's often the tipping point for success. Let me explain why I have this unconventional opinion.

People with impostor syndrome are successful. As previously mentioned, some of the most successful people in their respective fields have felt like imposters at some point in time, which may be very surprising to everyone else around them. They are just unable to process, internalize, or comprehend their own successes, but they are still objectively successful. The person who has a lucrative start-up business or graduated with multiple degrees and so on and so forth (however you want to define success) has still achieved all of those things even if he or she feels undeserving or unqualified. The rest of the world may not be able to comprehend how or why this person has impostor syndrome. How could they feel like an actual impostor if they are so successful? How someone perceives their own success may be vastly different from how the world views their success. While someone may be critical of themselves and feel like they are struggling, everyone else may see someone who is actually excelling. (Picture an image of the swan swimming gracefully on the water.) However, the inability to internalize success does not make someone unsuccessful nor devalue their accomplishments.

Most of the articles and blog posts out there on impostor syndrome highlight how individuals with impostor syndrome are usually some of the most successful people; however, these articles don't explain *why* individuals with impostorism were able to be successful in the first place. The focus was more on fixing problematic thinking and "overcoming" impostor syndrome, particularly in the workplace. This type of perspective doesn't acknowledge that self-proclaimed "frauds," "impostors," and "phonies" are actually doing a lot of things right. Even if they can't internalize their own achievements, these people share personal characteristics, inherent to impostor syndrome, that actually enable their current and future success in a world where being "unqualified" is becoming more normal. Systems and processes will continue to change due to technology, so it's impossible to always know how to do everything. The people who are used to feeling like they are operating outside of their comfort zones are in the position to thrive in this type of environment. They have the capabilities to continually excel and to help others excel as a strong leader in situations of uncertainty.

How did I determine the key components of the *impostor advantage*? In the survey I sent out to collect information on individual experiences with impostor syndrome, I asked survey takers what key personal attributes they believed were crucial to being successful. The following list includes the top four answers I received:

- Humility
- Flexibility / adaptability

- Perseverance / strong work ethic
- Emotional intelligence / empathy

Besides all being classified as "soft skills," these characteristics have something in common: All are fundamental to having impostor syndrome and being an "impostor." Let me give you a brief overview of how each attribute directly intersects with impostorism.

First, take humility. Humility is about showing modesty and humbleness toward your accomplishments. When someone attributes their own achievements or successes to luck, to good timing, or to someone providing them with a golden opportunity, they are exhibiting a kind of modesty toward their own capabilities and accomplishments. Impostors are humble people. Instead of saying, "I got this job because I am smart enough for the position," they say, "I was lucky I got this job because the recruiter liked me," or "I was fortunate to get this opportunity even though other candidates are probably more qualified than I am." They place more importance on external circumstances and luck than on their own talents or capabilities when analyzing why they were able to achieve something.

Next is flexibility or adaptability. Though impostors may feel underqualified or unfit in a certain setting, they are incredibly adaptive creatures. In recognizing they feel "out of place," they make it a priority to fit in with the rest of the group by acquiring the necessary knowledge to get there. They are professional chameleons. They blend in so much that other people see them as successful and well-adjusted people, even if they feel it is obvious to everyone else they are out of place or in over their head.

Strong work ethic and perseverance complement the previous characteristic of adaptability. Impostors will over-work, over-stress, over-prepare for presentations, and over-think in order to keep concealed that they actually do not feel prepared or completely confident in what they are doing. They tend to be perfectionists who go over the top to prove (mostly to themselves) they are indeed qualified. In an effort to get rid of the impostor feelings, they are willing to put in the extra work to feel they have the authentic knowledge that qualifies them for a particular role.

Lastly, we have emotional intelligence and empathy. Impostors understand what it means to feel like you are struggling to keep up, and they appreciate the process it takes to be successful. They understand it's not always glamorous and actually requires a lot of dedication and determination to succeed. They fully acknowledge that employees are not robots—they are real people who experience a range of emotions, including feelings of anxiety and uncertainty. This type of understanding allows people to become not only better team members but also better managers, as they know what may be on people's minds as they take on a new role and the encouragement they may want to hear.

The results of the survey I conducted confirmed my initial opinion that impostor syndrome can actually be a stepping-stone to success because being an "impostor" means having a set of traits or personal characteristics that are critical to success—the *impostor advantage*. *Impostor advantage* may seem like an unusual combination of words because of the negative connotation of the word "impostor." How can feeling like an "impostor" and struggling with authentic confidence be beneficial? The *impostor advantage* describes the positive edge, or rather the benefits, which can be created from having impostor syndrome and feeling like a "fraud." Though someone may have not felt qualified for the job or situation they are in, they have the personal qualifications to be successful through being an "impostor." Creating the *impostor advantage* requires self-awareness and self-reflection. To fully understand how to make the most out of impostor thoughts, it is important to determine why we feel like impostors in the first place. What surrounding factors trigger us to feel unqualified or unprepared? What attributes, qualifications, or achievements do we feel we are lacking? By recognizing both our strengths and our weaknesses simultaneously, we are able to feel more authentic in our existing capabilities and identify areas for potential growth. Recognizing impostor syndrome and developing the *impostor advantage* is an interactive process.

The next section of this book will dive further into the importance of each of these core attributes in the Digital Age and why "impostors" already have an advantage. While technology has encouraged impostor syndrome, it has also created working environments that require the personal characteristics that are inherent to impostor syndrome. With greater emphasis placed on soft skills—the attitude, mindset, emotional intelligence, and personality traits that someone brings to the table—"impostors" are positioned to succeed and to help those around them succeed as well. The rest of this book will continue to explore the components of the *impostor advantage*, how to leverage them in the Digital Age, and why feeling like an "impostor" is a crucial part to your own success story, whatever your definition of success may be.

PART II

From Syndrome to Success:
The Key Components of the *Impostor Advantage* in the Digital Age

CHAPTER 4

Professional Chameleons:

Adaptability and Impostor Syndrome

———

"Every single project I worked on I was required to be an expert at something I'd seen for only a few hours earlier that week."

—BANKING MANAGER, THIRTY-ONE, *IMPOSTOR SYNDROME SURVEY*

The ability to be a professional chameleon—to quickly learn and adapt—is more important than ever before.

In 2019 *Human Resource Executive*, an online publication that provides information on trends in talent management, released an article about whether soft skills are more important than the "right" qualifications. The article referenced a survey of two thousand adults conducted by Harris Poll, an American market research and analytics company, revealing that 75 percent of people would most likely hire a job candidate who has soft skills and not the right experience or qualifications if no "perfect" candidate existed. According to the survey, Americans would prefer candidates who displayed enthusiasm and willingness to learn over candidates with experience and poor personal skills.[16]

When you think about the skills essential for being "qualified" and having an advantage in the workplace in the Digital Age, it may seem logical to think of competencies that revolve around technology, including data analytics, data systems, project management, and a variety of other tech-related certifications. However, the development of disruptive technology, including automation and artificial intelligence, has caused individual roles, business models, and even entire industries to continually adapt to remain competitive. These types of changes require people to adapt too, as virtually every industry from healthcare and education to manufacturing and retail will be affected. Though it is difficult to know exactly what the job market will look like in 2030, it is certain that some jobs will be displaced entirely and new opportunities will emerge due to unknown cutting-edge technology and the streamlined processes it creates.[17] Ten years ago, there were no job postings for digital marketing managers, UX designers, or Cloud computing specialists. These integral new roles were created in response to technology. Ten years from now, there will likely be many new roles that reflect recent innovations. How can someone be prepared with the right skills for technology that doesn't even exist yet?

16   Michael O'Brien, "Are Soft Skills More Important than the Right Qualifications?" *Human Resource Executive,* Sussex Publishers, March 12, 2019.

17   James Manyika et al., "Harnessing automation for a future that works," *McKinsey Global Institute,* January 12, 2017.

As technology replaces activities we can easily replicate and repeat, the workforce will focus on activities that require higher levels of cognitive thinking. The basis for success at work has and will continue to place a greater emphasis on soft skills, including learnability, communication, teamwork, problem solving, and emotional intelligence. These types of skills do not become obsolete over time as new technology is introduced; in fact, they become more important to sustain, as they can often be challenged and hindered by technology.

* * *

As a DevOps engineer responsible for delivering software changes, Scott's career has been driven by technological change and his willingness to adapt to it.

> *The amount of change in my field is the reason I have been able to be successful. One of the biggest things in my field right now is called Kubernetes. The technology was released by Google in 2014, and now nearly every Fortune 500 company uses it. No one has ten to fifteen years of experience in it because it is so new, so even if you have two years of experience you are considered the "expert." In technology, there's always a new framework or a new way to do something.*

Scott learned Kubernetes through a combination of self-teaching and on-the-job experience. He now has a skill that is listed on thousands of open job listings on LinkedIn. In this case, Scott's willingness to adapt to a new way of working has made him an attractive candidate on the job market. Though operating in a field that experiences regular change, his ability to understand a current industry need and pick it up quickly enabled his success. Scott's story shows there is a high probability of facing unknown territory while working in tech, which may cause someone to feel like they are unprepared or unqualified as they must learn a new process, system, or methodology.

Though experience in fast-paced fields may trigger feelings of impostor syndrome, the ways in which "impostors" are able to analyze and quickly adapt to their surroundings is an invaluable skill in the Digital Age.

In November 2019, I sat in a coffee shop on M Street in Georgetown talking with a college student about her interest in management consulting. She wanted me to discuss what a day in the life of a consultant was truly like and if my college classes had prepared me for the transition from late nights in the library to late nights in the office. When I thought about how to describe my work experience, I got an image in my head of being thrown into the deep end of a swimming pool and having to quickly find my way to the surface. My job felt like a continuous adrenaline rush. Part of the "thrill" of working in the industry is the slight terror mixed with excitement that you get when you are assigned a new task or project in a completely unfamiliar subject area. You have days (maybe weeks, if you're lucky) to become an "expert" on the subject of the engagement and understand the complexity of the business environment to put together an impressive presentation for your new client. Since no project is exactly the same, the beginning of each assignment means spending some quality time researching and browsing client documentation after hours and on the weekends to figure out the lay of the land for the next eight to ten weeks. I equally loved and hated this particular aspect of my job. I loved to be challenged and I loved to learn, but I hated to feel unsure and uncertain if I was prepared on each new project.

Usually, when I finally felt comfortable with the work of a project and could feel knowledgeable speaking about it, it was time to wrap up and move on to the next engagement and the next client. The short-term satisfaction of completing a project is overshadowed by the unknown of the next assignment. That is the life of a consultant—a never-ending cycle of "getting up to speed." Quite honestly, I felt like I had chosen to become an impostor by profession. Though at some point consultants develop competencies within a given industry, each project or engagement has its own unique set of challenges.

When you have the type of job that presents new assignments and new situations to solve on a regular basis, it is easy to fall into a thinking pattern that you may not be prepared or don't have enough knowledge to be successful. This is because with each new challenge at work you have to confront the fact that you may not know exactly how to do something and will have to figure it out as you go. You can use your past experiences as a framework for your approach, but there is always the risk that this might not be enough to solve the problem at hand. Though often what may seem like a stressful new project is actually a new opportunity for growth and a learning experience in disguise.

The ability to relabel an overwhelming challenge at work to a "learning opportunity" starts with mindset.

Carol Dweck, Professor of Psychology at Stanford University and author of the book *Mindset: The New Psychology of*

Success, has explored the two predominant mindsets people exhibit as they navigate life, fixed and growth, and how these mindsets are linked to an individual's potential for success. A fixed mindset believes that intelligence or talent is something static while a growth mindset believes that intelligence or talent is something that can be developed over time. A fixed mindset prefers to avoid obstacles and challenges, while a growth mindset embraces challenges and the experience that they provide. Individuals with a fixed mindset put preference on "looking smart" versus wanting to learn, which can inhibit the potential for success, as fixed mindset individuals are avoiding the challenging opportunities that would help further develop their talents. By focusing too much on confirming and affirming their own abilities as they are, people who exhibit a fixed mindset are sacrificing time to develop those abilities. Growth mindset is cultivated in organizations that allow and encourage risk-taking with the understanding that even more lessons can be learned from failure than from success. Dweck supports that personal improvement occurs when you take risks and operate just outside of your comfort zone. This makes complete sense. Hypothetically, if you want to advance your career, each stepping-stone or new job should be slightly more challenging than the last. You have the basic qualifications to be successful in the new position, but there will undoubtedly be new skills you will have to learn as you take on the role. Similar to progressing through school years, the knowledge you learned in each grade was necessary to advance to the next grade and then build off that existing knowledge.[18]

---

18   Carol Dweck, "What Having a "Growth Mindset" Actually Means," *Harvard Business Review*, January 13, 2016.

I think why so many post-college, young adults experience impostor syndrome is because, like me, they thought to some extent when they graduated from college and got settled into their careers that the period of tremendous learning would stop and life would be stable in some way. We associated adulthood with a break from learning. When we sold back our last textbooks, we may have been closing the chapter on the school stage, but the learning stage was very much not over yet. The diploma was not just an indication of all what was learned in college but also a sign of being more or less prepared to start the next phase of learning in adulthood by starting a career. In retrospect, the most learning I did happened after I graduated when I learned how to navigate real life and real responsibilities. The learning curve continues well into your twenties even though the ways in which our knowledge is tested has changed. Though I didn't have to take final exams anymore or pull all-nighters in the campus library to finish the paper that I took too long to start, I still had to prepare for demonstrations of my own knowledge to my managers and clients in the form of deliverables and presentations.

In the midst of the 2020 pandemic, my friend Dan switched jobs. He went from working in the accounting department at a food services company to being a financial consultant for a well-known healthcare IT company. Suddenly, he was launched into morning conference calls listening to concepts he had never heard before in what he described as a "trial by fire" transition into his new (virtual) working environment. At first the tech jargon and steep learning curve made Dan experience an "oh shit, am I not cut out for this?" moment.

Months later I asked Dan what he did to adapt so quickly to a new role, new workplace culture, and new industry.

What truly helped for me was to take a step back and put some perspective into it. I realized rather than focus on what I don't know, I should take what I do know and apply it to what I'm trying to learn, as well as accept the fact that I don't know everything. It really gave me the ability to dive in headfirst. So rather than just pushing a request through just focusing on my part of it, I took extra steps along the way to ask questions to at least get a base understanding of the product, service, software, whatever it may be. I was jumping into any and every meeting I could get an invite to as a way to learn on the fly, which had a great response from my fellow associates because it showed I truly cared and wanted to learn as much as possible to help the team in the best way I could.

The ability of "impostors" to adapt to new jobs, new roles, or new projects by learning new skills is a key component of the *impostor advantage*. Their ability to shift quickly makes them a valuable asset to their team as they hit the ground running on projects. It also positions them to excel as leaders who can assess changes to their surrounding environment and adjust their strategy accordingly. They are not afraid to learn and adapt on the fly. Technology increases uncertainty in the Digital Age, as the ways in which we work are constantly changing. Employees must be able to adapt to continuous learning, and the constant development of skills as business processes persistently change to maximize operational efficiency—skills that were not part of their college curriculum. Consider how many people are attaining jobs that may outwardly seem misaligned with what they studied in college. I was surprised when I realized how many non-finance or business majors were employed within the financial services consulting practice at my firm, but this is a common occurrence across many industries, as an individual's ability to learn and problem solve is sometimes more valued than the classes they took in undergrad.

The focus on learning and talent development is further evidenced by the level of spending by corporations on internal training programs, which averaged at eighty-four billion dollars from 2016 to 2018, showing a sixteen-billion-dollar increase from the prior three-year average. Companies understand the value of investing in their own people to cultivate the types of skills and competencies they need. As the automation of basic processes continues at a rapid pace and skillsets become obsolete in a matter of years, re-skilling is an essential reality for employers and employees. The capacity to adapt and to learn is inevitability becoming equally, if not more, important than previously established knowledge.[19]

Impostor syndrome may seem to align to a fixed mindset, as it is rooted in the fear of being revealed as an impostor or a phony and wanting to appear smart and confident. Due to an obsession with exhibiting competence, there is a potential consequence that someone may limit their own potential if they believe they have gotten to where they are based on luck. They will not be motivated to progress to the next stepping-stone in their professional or academic career, as the next step may seem like even more out of their comfort zone. Individuals may even develop a fear of success, because success may mean more visibility and additional responsibilities when someone demonstrates they are capable of performing. Because individuals who have

---

19   Patricia Duchene, "The Evolving Workplace," *Forbes*, March 13, 2019.

impostor syndrome want to avoid failure at all costs, they tend to fall into unhealthy work habits as they strive for an unattainable perfection. When the task at hand is completed and some sort of validation or praise is received, the person with impostor syndrome then gives credit to the intense preparation that occurred. As in "I nailed this presentation with the client because I stayed up until 2 a.m. the night before it was due fine-tuning the formatting and practicing talking points." Even if the individual would have performed the same way if they had gone to sleep at 11 p.m., they have begun to convince themselves that they have to work harder, maybe even sacrifice their own personal lives, in order to achieve and succeed, which creates a negative perception that success means giving up part of your own wellbeing.

The fixed mindset prevents someone from seeing that these types of "crunch time" experiences actually allow for personal growth and the development of abilities. Each challenge to be faced or problem to be solved provides a valuable learning experience. However, impostor syndrome and the growth mindset is a powerful combination, which leads to the *impostor advantage.* The person who can identify their own improvement areas while understanding they can expand their knowledge has unlimited growth potential. This shift in mindset embraces the advantages of feeling like an impostor, because what may seem like a personal limitation is actually a sign of the potential for success when someone exhibits the willingness to adapt to a new or changed environment despite the insecurities they may have. The *impostor advantage* is rooted in a growth mindset that welcomes learning and change without the fear of revealing knowledge gaps. The *impostor advantage* mindset accepts it is nearly impossible to know everything that you will encounter as you take on new kinds of responsibilities. The last section of this book will explain what "embracing" impostor syndrome looks like and why accepting the *impostor advantage* can radically improve how you approach future situations of uncertainty.

CHAPTER 5

The Benefits of Overthinking:

Emotional Intelligence and Impostor Syndrome

———

I abruptly got off the phone after receiving a small bit of "critical feedback." After working a few fourteen-plus-hour days in a row, honestly the last thing that I wanted to hear was how I messed up and could have done something better. Even though my mistake was not truly that important in the big scheme of things—it was not presented in a leadership meeting or widely distributed in an email—my voice started to grow quiet and shaky.

When I initially stepped away from my desk to go make myself a cup of tea, I felt guilty that I got emotional on the phone and embarrassed that I had appeared imperfect. Later that night after I had wrapped up for the day, I replayed the conversation in my head. My initial feelings of guilt began to fade away. I thought that my manager had been aware of the fact that I had been putting in many hours and was approaching complete exhaustion, but suddenly I came to the realization that, really, no one else truly understood the sheer amount of "paddling" I was doing under the surface. Only *I* knew that (and the couple of friends who had let me speak candidly). The fact that I was so emotionally invested in my work indicated the amount of time and effort I had contributed recently. I changed my perspective on the whole situation. I began to tell myself that I was *allowed* to feel upset and to feel tired. More importantly, I was *allowed* to make mistakes sometimes.

These types of learning experiences, which have happened a couple of times in my career, often make me reflect on the type of manager and leader I want to be. One of the largest complaints I hear from friends and colleagues when they express discontent about work is that they feel their managers and bosses do not show empathy or understanding. They want their superiors to recognize them as a person with a life and priorities outside of work, and not just an employee who is on-call all the time, a reality that has become all too true for people who have seen work-life balance disappear during the COVID pandemic. Understanding the emotional needs of the team is important for creating a compassionate environment where people can feel safe expressing their opinions, being imperfect, and displaying their "humanness." Emotional intelligence and empathy have major benefits in the workplace in addition to employees feeling more valued or appreciated. A corporate culture where people feel comfortable being vulnerable enables the kind of diversity in perspective that promotes innovative problem-solving. Additionally, emotional intelligence is a capability that is very difficult to replicate with technology, making it a continued priority for hiring managers.

* * *

Since its application to the business world several decades ago, "emotional intelligence" has no doubt become a popular corporate buzzword in leadership workshops and a decisive factor for hiring managers and recruiters as they evaluate potential candidates. Objectively, teaching a new hire how to use the company's data management system is easier than trying to teach them how to operate with emotional intelligence. It is an aptitude that will never be replaced by a robot and is crucial to the internal and external relationship-building in business. Empathy, a core component for emotional intelligence, is at the foundation for entrepreneurship, as it involves identifying human needs and creating a business to support those. Though your emotional quotient (EQ) score doesn't have its own line on your resumé like a GPA or GRE score, the possession of this ability (or "skill") holds equal significance to the technical skills listed. Emotional intelligence is not only about learning how to understand and manage your own emotions, but also about understanding and managing the emotions of the people around you. In their 2017 article on the twelve elements of emotional intelligence (EI), Daniel Goleman and Richard Boyatzis classified EI into four broad domains: self-awareness, self-management, social awareness, and relationship management. Self-awareness was the starting point for enhanced emotional intelligence.[20]

Dr. Lilly Roy, a scientist working in the pharmaceutical industry in Boston, sat down with me (virtually) to talk about her own experiences with impostor syndrome. She had a

20   Daniel Goleman and Richard Boyatzis, "Emotional Intelligence Has 12 Elements. Which Do You Need to Work On?" Harvard Business Review, December 5, 2017.

few examples at her current role, and she really noticed EQ coming up when she was starting a fitness coaching business. Being in tune with her emotional intelligence was critical to her journey. She explained how encountering new experiences can trigger fear-based emotions related to our past—usually, past events which caused us to feel unsafe. These fear-based emotions can create resistance to action, and facing these emotions and triggers head on is critical for success.

> *If you are taking on new roles or a new business—constantly going after it—you are triggering emotions in yourself. Patterns come back when you are about to level up. Whenever you are going to expand yourself, you need to expand your own emotional intelligence.*

Dr. Roy highlighted that it was "inner work" that allowed her to be okay with the rejection she may experience when starting a new business in an area outside of her normal comfort zone. This was also key when taking on new opportunities at work that could lead to perceived failure, particularly if the opportunity is highly visible. She stressed the importance of inner work to evaluate your own reactions to people and situations in order to be successful and lead successful teams. Dr. Roy now helps other women elevate their own emotional intelligence.

> *Emotions may be difficult to speak about in a corporate setting. The people who are really successful are going back to questions such as "Why am I being reactive?" and "Why am I not letting go?"*

The emotionally intelligent do the inner work to identify their own triggers. For example, when triggered, they take the time to ask, "What does this remind me of?" or "When is the last time I felt like this, and what was going on?" Simply bringing awareness to the trigger and recognizing they could be projecting their past onto their present can sometimes be enough to release it. It's also important to be aware that other people might have the same kinds of triggers. She emphasized that people who experience impostor syndrome often are taking on a new task without the support they need to be successful. Taking time to identify your perceived gaps and pursuing mentorship or support to fill those gaps can make a big difference. Reframing to yourself that "this is not hard; it is just new" can help to confront thoughts patterns that are creating resistance to act. Lastly, expect the need to hone in on your own emotional intelligence when you are about to "level up," such as starting a new venture or taking on a new role.

Capgemini Research Institute published findings in 2020 on why emotional intelligence is a critical skillset in a world that continues to progress artificial intelligence (AI) technologies. The study concluded that over the next three to five years there would be a five times or greater increase in demand for employees with high levels of emotional intelligence in the following sectors: financial services, automotive, retail, consumer products, and utilities. This is because the shift of easily replicated processes to automation in these industries will mean that the remaining roles (that cannot be automated) will require employees to have the cognitive skills and awareness to adapt to changing work environments. Organizations greatly benefit from hiring and retaining employees with higher levels of emotional intelligence. Benefits include enhanced productivity, high employee satisfaction, increased market share, and reduced attrition.[21] The positive impacts for the company are both internal and external, as people with emotional intelligence are able to form strong professional relationships that enable team success as well as deliver products and services that consider the needs of customers or clients.

Before we get into how feeling like an impostor is helpful in becoming an emotionally intelligent person in the Digital Age, let's consider how technology has impacted some of the elements. Emotional intelligence is a highly valued attribute, but has one of its main components, empathy, been under attack in the Digital Age? Is it truly possible for empathy to exist online? Technology has created quite the paradox. We are clearly more connected to other people than ever before as we stay Facebook friends with people from our past and are able to do business with people across the world in different time zones. At the same time, we are becoming more isolated and more distant as a global population because it has become more difficult to connect on a deeper level. Several potential reasons for this distancing of human connection exist. With so much information available at all times, between blogs, social media, and online news sources, the information over-load regularly bombards internet users with unpleasant news, which can make us feel desensitized or completely emotion-ally exhausted, which we may not even fully recognize. At times, social media can be a powerful tool to foster empathy and garner support for causes with the high visibility, but never without some form of controversy or disagreement expressed by opposing viewpoints. Though the internet is a source of information from a multitude of perspectives, the

---

21   Capgemini Research Institute, Emotional Intelligence Research, Executive Survey, August–September 2019.

types of information that people read and view online are usually curated to their own existing beliefs. Political media outlets entrench party lines by creating forums where people who have the same ideologies reinforce each other without outside interpretation. You can easily scroll over thoughts that you don't believe in and completely ignore another person's perspective on a matter, only choosing to read those articles that agree with your thoughts and values. In fact, there are entire algorithms on social media, including those used by Facebook and Instagram, dedicated to showing content that would be appealing to you because it is largely in line with your existing beliefs. Our search history and online activities almost scarily impact the types of information that appears in our feeds, making it easy to continually reinforce our existing opinions.[22]

Beside information bias created online, empathy has been impacted by the ways in which people interact virtually. Online interactions simply cannot completely replicate or replace in-person interactions. Our brains are programmed to be in-person when interacting with other people. During interactions, the human brain has emotional centers in the subcortex that receive information from the other person based on facial cues and conversation tone and then determine how to respond in an appropriate manner. The prefrontal cortex includes circuits that are meant to control emotional responses that may cause the interaction to take a negative turn. A part of the brain called the supramarginal gyrus is responsible for detecting a lack of empathy in ourselves and course correcting. When conversations and interactions happen online or over the phone without video,

22 "How Do Social Media Algorithms Work?" Digital Marketing Institute, May 3, 2019.

the brain does not receive the same cues to create an empathetic response since eye contact is missing. It is difficult to fully understand what the person is thinking or feeling without observing them physically. People must solely rely on what the person is saying versus what they are showing or feeling in order to determine if an empathetic response is needed. With that being said, people are more likely to express less-than thoughtful words via text, email, or even phone call because the feedback cycle that occurs in the brain during an in-person interaction to control impulsive words or action is no longer present. In general, it is also just more difficult to understand what someone is feeling when they say something without body language cues. Say you ask your friend if they want to grab drinks after work. If they respond an "okay" that isn't followed by an emoji smiley face, you might wonder if they are secretly mad at you. Misinterpretations and over-analyzation of text communication is just unavoidable.[23]

Like a muscle that needs to be exercised, empathy is something to build up and then continually practice in order to maintain. Certain parts of the brain, known as the default mode network, are linked to the learning and development of empathy, and interestingly enough, these brain functions are activated when a person is not doing anything at all—when they are not engaged with other people, laptops, or mobile devices. This seems like a rarity nowadays, as we are almost always plugged in and staring at a screen when we are not sleeping. When the brain is not stimulated by external factors and distractions, it is able to focus on internal thoughts,

---

23   Christopher Bergland, "The Neuroscience of Empathy," *Psychology Today,* Sussex Publishers, October 10, 2013.

feelings, and memories. The idle or "daydreaming" state of the brain is how people develop their ability to have empathy, since empathy is tied to an imaginative mindset—being able to imagine yourself in another person's situation and to be introspective about your own past experiences.[24]

Besides imagination and introspection, empathy is also centered on vulnerability—accepting the vulnerability of others and showing your own vulnerability. Social media platforms create a forum for individuals to share aspects of their lives with others, which may include showing moments of imperfection or weakness. It can be difficult to demonstrate vulnerability online when we can't exactly predict how other people will react and when we cannot see their reactions. We do not have the comfort of another person showing us support or consolation, more than lines of text, when we reveal something that may be difficult to express. However, Brené Brown, a professor of social work who created a TEDx Talk on the power of vulnerability that received over forty million views, said, "In order for connection to happen, we have to allow ourselves to be seen—really seen."[25]

Dr. Lilly Roy and I also discussed the advantages of being vulnerable online to establish a sense of community.

"People who are brave enough to be vulnerable in the right way and with the right people find a lot of benefit," added Dr. Roy.

24   Patrícia Oliveira Silva et al., "Empathy by Default: Correlates in the Brain at Rest," *Psicothema* 30, no. 1 (2018): 97-103. doi: 10.7334/psicothema2016.366

25   Brené, Brown, 2010, "The Power of Vulnerability," Filmed June 2010 in Houston, Texas, TED video, 20:03.

Despite the challenges of developing emotional intelligence in a very digital world, people who have impostor syndrome have the predisposition to develop high emotional intelligence and to use that emotional intelligence to excel in both their personal and professional lives through self-awareness and social awareness. Why is this the case? Well, firstly, self-proclaimed impostors are highly self-aware. They fully acknowledge what they do know and what they don't know with an emphasis on the latter. They are maybe even too self-aware when they get to the point of being overly critical. They constantly analyze their own qualifications against what qualifications they believe they need in order to successfully accomplish a task or to execute a role. When an impostor takes on a new position or a new task, they evaluate their own abilities against what they believe are the prerequisites of the position or task to determine if they are qualified. As professionals of the personal gap analysis, they compare themselves to colleagues, fellow students, and peers to determine where they measure up and where they are lacking. Though impostor syndrome is negatively associated with overpreparation, overworking, and overthinking, these behaviors associated with impostor syndrome are actually very important to having the type of introspection that is necessary to being in-tune with one's own strengths and weaknesses.

As emotional intelligence begins with self-awareness, impostor syndrome also starts with a heightened sense of self-awareness of someone's own capabilities. Self-awareness is exhibited when someone admits to themselves that they have applied to a job that they are not objectively qualified for or that they are not knowledgeable about a subject area that is significant to their job. Self-awareness is also the groundwork for being able to have empathy for other people and to have social awareness. In order to be able to relate and provide compassion to someone else, there first has to be some understanding of self and the experiences that have shaped us as people. Impostors are inclined to exhibit empathy as they understand the process, if not struggle, of feeling not good enough and not belonging. They also take the introspection time to reflect on their own experiences when they delve into self-awareness. Though people with impostor syndrome may need to consider how to express greater empathy to themselves by being kinder and more understanding when they make mistakes, they will be empathetic in a managerial role as they understand the pressure that someone else may feel when they are assigned an unfamiliar task. They may create an atmosphere of open communication that emphasizes there are "no stupid questions." They may even be more in-tune with the types of motivation to give so that a person feels supported and not terrified to fail when they feel uncertain. An impostor can leverage their own personal experiences to put themselves in someone else's shoes and ensure that the other person feels supported.

When someone is able to provide empathy to someone else based on this understanding and shared vulnerabilities, they can feel more connected. This is the type of connection that we cannot let fade away in the Digital Age, even though technology can make it more difficult. Social awareness and empathy toward other people are becoming ever so important as society faces new challenges together, including fights for justice and global pandemics. It's important to not lose the "human aspect" in the office, as work and the roles we fill there are just one aspect of our lives, identities, and success. As humans are innately social beings, emotional intelligence is crucial to both personal and professional success. Intelligence by itself will not bring success if it is not supported by emotional intelligence and consideration for other people. Desired skills in the Digital Age will continue to evolve to be that which technology can never provide—the human perspective. Emotional intelligence is not just a buzzword but a necessity for navigating today's world. Feeling like an impostor—and understanding that others may feel like impostors—is a great start to expanding your own emotional intelligence.

CHAPTER 6

The Power of "I Don't Know":

Intellectual Humility and Impostor Syndrome

———

Saying "I don't know" out loud is difficult—I'll admit it.

Those three words essentially vanish from the vocabulary of prospective candidates as they enter job interviews and want to display that they know as much as possible in their respective fields. Why? Because it's uncomfortable to display a knowledge gap. If there is something they don't know yet—the answer to a question, a methodology, or a type of system or software— they may start to panic about coming across as "unqualified." Then they stress to the hiring manager their ability to learn and absorb rapidly to make up for this "weakness."

Saying "I don't know" in your head is much easier...and something people with impostor syndrome do frequently.

There is something powerful about admitting to others or to yourself that you don't know something. Intellectual humility is the next key component of the *impostor advantage.*

* * *

It's no secret that humility is a key ingredient to success.

During a 2012 campaign appearance in Roanoke, Virginia, soon-to-be reelected President Barack Obama delivered some comments later seen as somewhat controversial. This is what he said:

> *If you've been successful, you didn't get there on your own. I'm always struck by people who think, well, it must be because I was just so smart. There are a lot of smart people out there. It must be because I worked harder than everybody else. Let me tell you something— there are a whole bunch of hardworking people out there. If you were successful, somebody along the line gave you some help.... If you've got a business, you didn't build that. Somebody else made that happen.*[26]

Though this speech didn't necessarily go over well with businessmen in Virginia, President Obama was delivering an important point about success and humility. He was emphasizing that success is never an individual endeavor and is instead the result of collective efforts. Humility is the cognizance that success is not a solo act.

Humility has been challenged by the Digital Age. Technology has distorted modesty, as social media platforms have

---

26   President Barack Obama, (speech, campaign event, Roanoke, Virginia, July 13, 2012).

largely normalized a culture of bragging and boasting about personal accomplishments. Why do people even have Facebook, Instagram, or Twitter in the first place? To share their own highlight reel or achievements with the rest of the world, or at least their base of followers. Social media accounts encourage individualism. It's not uncommon for someone to create a lengthy post about an award they received or about a new job acceptance. The "humble brag" has become a popular way to disguise displays of personal accomplishments. This is a completely unique phenomenon to the Digital Age. Generations before social media generally did not reserve space in the local newspaper or hang signs around to announce their accomplishments. This level of self-aggrandizement was just simply not done until there were platforms that made money off of encouraging people to talk and share about themselves in a very public manner. LinkedIn was created so people could share their professional and academic achievements with their network. It is encouraged to play up your image on LinkedIn to attract the right networking opportunities and even recruiters. Today's online environment seems to imply that if you aren't out promoting yourself, you are probably not getting noticed. (Though if you feel a little bit awkward self-marketing and talking about your own accomplishments online, that's probably a good sign. More to come on that later.) The hyper-focus on self-confidence and self-promotion can breed competitiveness and cause individuals to only think about what is best for their own career marketability.

Ironically, in a society where humility may be consistently challenged, it has become even more important to have humility in the workplace. Why is that? Humility, the quality of not showing excessive pride in your own abilities and beliefs, is irreplaceable. As increased digitalization and disruptive technology takes over a large portion of jobs across industries, higher-level cognitive thinking and emotional know-how will remain as important skills that cannot be duplicated or made obsolete. According to Professor Ed Hess, who authored *Humility Is the New Smart: Rethinking Human Excellence in the Smart Machine Age*, a large ego is limiting in the age of smart machines and rapid innovation. An overstated sense of self will hinder success in certain areas, which include problem solving, innovative thinking, and creativity, all of which require a sense of humility. Having a big ego prevents someone from being able to fully accept alternative ideas or imagine someone else's situation in order to create a solution that is meaningful for a variety of people. Professor Hess explains that learning to shut off our own egos actually goes against human nature, because our brains work in a way that seeks out and selects confirming information. This means that we look for information that affirms our existing beliefs, and we tend to be defensive about those beliefs as well. Hess also conjectured that success requires owning your mistakes and mishaps, being open to ideas that disagree with your own, and understanding that the best ideas may not always being your own. All of these actions are underpinned by a sense of humility. Hess argues that humility is required to stay relevant into the future because self-promotion is not sustainable. People who demonstrate the capacity for collaboration and teamwork, and the elevated levels of thinking that are associated with both, will be the most desired thinkers in a world with automated intelligence that is not capable of such activities. Innovation and critical thinking are driven by people who are open-minded, comfortable with having their own ideas challenged, and curious to find out *what* is the best solution instead of *who* has the best solution.[27]

Humility is essential to not only being a successful team member but also being a successful leader of a team. It requires an understanding of your own strengths and weaknesses and how they can be balanced with the strengths and weaknesses of others. A study conducted by the Global Center for Digital Business Transformation revealed that leadership characteristics between disruptive environments with high levels of innovation and stable environments (less innovation) are mostly similar but have several important differences.[28] There is a need for greater humility in leadership in disruptive environments. With all of the complexity, rapid changes, and unknowns in today's world, the most successful leaders and people are those who can put aside their preconceived notions and ways of working to make room for greater efficiencies. A humble leader will break down limiting notions of hierarchy that may prevent younger team members from contributing ideas and insights, because they understand the value of an "all hands on deck" approach to develop innovative solutions. They understand that knowledge and the ability to provide a beneficial perspective is not solely based on years of experience.

So what is the connection between impostor syndrome and humility?

Impostors are humble. They express modesty toward their own accomplishments and achievements both in the office and in their personal lives. The Dunning-Kruger effect

---

27   Edward Hess, "Humility: The No. 1 Job Skill Needed for the Smart Machine Age," *Forbes,* May 18, 2015.

28   Terry Bennett, "Humility Required for Digital Era Success," *Institute for Digital Transformation,* June 15, 2018.

explores the connection between impostor syndrome and humility. The concept was first developed by two Cornell psychologists, David Dunning and Justin Kruger, when they tested participants on three areas: logic, grammar, and sense of humor. They noticed that the participants who performed in the bottom quartile actually thought they performed well above the average due to issues with metacognition, or "the ability to analyze one's own thoughts or performance." The leading cause of the Dunning-Kruger effect, which is often called the polar opposite of impostor syndrome, was attributed to society having an over-emphasis on confidence. People value looking smart, even if they are pretending, rather than admitting they don't know something. This effect is more than just about perceived intelligence. Even highly intelligent people can experience it when they try to convince themselves their abilities can be transferred across multiple areas. Intelligence, however, is not a substitute for learning a new skill. The results of the study showed that more competent people who scored higher on the areas tested underestimated their own performance even after they were shown evidence of their success. The high performers expressed humility toward their own abilities.[29]

Instead of attributing individual successes to hard work, talent, or capabilities, impostors attribute their achievements to luck, opportune timing, and any other rationalization that does not include crediting themselves. There is some truth in this kind of thinking, as illustrated in President Obama's speech. Some parts of our successes are attributed to our own talents or abilities, even if we try to downplay that part, but there are other factors that help to bring about each one

29   "Dunning-Kruger Effect," *Psychology Today*, Sussex Publishers.

of our achievements. Take the example of graduating from college. Yes, you are the one who went to class, pulled a few all-nighters, took final exams, and then ultimately received the diploma at the end of the four years. However, you can recognize that this achievement was more than just your own. It was also your parents or grandparents paying for your tuition or supporting you in some way emotionally or financially while you focused on your work, your professors for being available to help you embrace new concepts, and the friends who made sure that you got home safely to your dorm from the campus bar. There was a series of events and a group of people who contributed in various ways to help you get that expensive piece of paper that hopefully you have framed somewhere.

Humility is an understanding of this type of interconnectivity and an appreciation for each of the details, like looking at a painting and noticing each of the individual brush strokes and how they blend together to make the whole scene. Maybe a single brush stroke of color on its own is not impressive, but a collection of colors is a work of art. This book is the result of multiple groups of people who helped turn the topic from an idea to a printed paperback—a professor who gave me the opportunity to write a book and helped me refine the topic scope, multiple editors who reviewed my writing and provided feedback, a marketing team that helped me develop a publishing campaign and design a book cover, other authors who shared their own experiences, and supportive friends and family who motivated me to continue writing even when I started to question myself. The book you are reading would not have made it through the entire publishing process if any one of these groups was not involved. To me, being humble is accepting that everything I am able to accomplish is a collection of efforts that are not all my own.

The humble mindset of impostor syndrome encourages gratitude. If someone feels they have gotten to a certain place in life (say, landing their dream job) because they are just really "lucky" and not because of the type of employee that they are, then they are more likely to be grateful about what they do have in the moment. Even though my job stresses me out on a daily basis because sometimes I feel like I'm being told to steer a ship after only receiving one lesson on the water, I can't help but feel overwhelmingly grateful for where I am. This is what drives impostors to work harder and to create a sense of belonging, because they are cognizant of what they have and what they want to hold on to. For that reason, they urgently want to prove to themselves and to others that they deserve what they have received. Impostors may be absolutely terrified of messing up when they've been assigned something that is way out of their comfort zone, but they do an excellent job of not showing that fear to other people, especially their managers.

The hard work and the paddling to keep up with the current always happens under the surface. I want to feel that I am capable of navigating the waters on my own, so I will put in the extra hours and do whatever I need to do to get to that level of comfort. Still stressful? Absolutely. But there is something really empowering about being able to look back and say, "Wow, I thought I was never going to feel confident in my work, and I did the damn thing anyway," even if that's just a temporary feeling until the next challenge comes along. Being grateful allows me to make the most of the opportunity at hand, even when it seems overwhelming.

Humility allows for empathy, as it encourages someone to think about others in addition to themselves. Similar to emotional intelligence, self-awareness is at the foundation of humility. Humility is honest self-perception and acknowledgment of what you don't already know, which may seem counterintuitive in a society that encourages showcasing our strengths and keeping our weaknesses private. Social media is often used to show what we do know, but not the areas of knowledge where we are lacking. No one posts on LinkedIn "I know nothing about project management," or "I struggled at work today because I don't know how to create a v-lookup in Excel." At least *I* definitely have not seen any posts like these on my feed. We don't want people to view us as unskilled or incompetent, especially if we are just starting out in our careers, so we have become marketers of our own personal brand.

Ayesha Noelle is an impostor syndrome coach based out of the Netherlands who helps female entrepreneurs address impostor syndrome and embrace their own visibility. Ayesha speaks about the kind of rhetoric that enforces the pressure to know everything. Over a Zoom call one morning, she discussed with me an important distinction in how we classify our own knowledge.

"There is a difference between being an 'expert' versus a 'lifetime learner with expertise,'" she told me.

Ayesha explained that an expert is someone who knows everything about a certain topic, whereas the lifetime learner acknowledges they have expertise in a certain area but are continually learning as well. Through this distinction, Ayesha helps her clients to acknowledge their own capabilities and to feel comfortable with being "visible" at work without fear of the perceptions of the others. I think we may put a lot of pressure on ourselves when we list a certain type of skill or qualification on our resumes that we have to know absolutely everything about the topic or else we're an "impostor" for even listing it. This type of thinking doesn't recognize that knowledge isn't just a simple check box. Intellectual humility is the ability to recognize your current level of knowledge and identify where you have the opportunity to learn more, simultaneously. There is power in admitting what you don't know something or where you have room to grow to others or to yourself. In fact, recognizing what you don't know is a strength, because it allows you to self-identify areas for improvement, a starting point for embracing a growth mindset.

What does intellectual humility look like in the Digital Age?

Intellectual humility is acknowledging the potential for confirmation bias online or searching for information that only affirms your existing beliefs and allowing yourself to question and reevaluate your own beliefs. It is not a sign of weakness to change your mind or to develop a new view-point, because there are always so many different perspectives to consider on any given topic. Intellectual humility also means that although you have access to an over-abundance of information online, you can accept that you will not know everything, nor are you expected to know everything all at once. This self-awareness allows you to focus on what you do know, your strengths, while developing an understanding of what you still need to learn. The inner impostor or the inner questioning voice provides the humility to be the type of open-minded, innovative thinker that is heavily sought after in the Digital Age.

The final section of this book will provide tips on how to leverage intellectual humility for personal growth in situations where you may be experiencing impostor syndrome— saying "I don't know" is the first step.

CHAPTER 7

Just Keep Swimming:

Perseverance and Impostor Syndrome

———

Imagine you have just hit mile three of a particularly difficult six-mile hike. You're not looking at the trees behind you, and instead your eyes are focused on the peak of the steep mountain that you're currently climbing. Impostor syndrome is like being at that halfway point and saying, "Wow—look at how much farther I have to go," instead of "Wow—look how far I have come," then continuing to climb.

Etahjayne knows the hard work and perseverance that it takes to succeed. She has worked in the fast-paced, high-stakes environment of a big corporate law firm for the last two and a half years. As an associate attorney, Etahjayne's experience includes representing corporate clients in their litigation needs by providing plans of action to respond to business claims. However, her day-to-day is not always predictable, and she is often faced with tough, unfamiliar cases that can cause her to examine her own capabilities. Etahjayne explained to me how working in a field that consistently presents new challenges (and opportunities to learn) can make every day feel like the first day of a new job.

Some days I feel like I just started even though it's been nearly three years now. I have been receiving more responsibility and more difficult assignments. Though it's nerve-wracking, it also shows that there is trust in me that I can handle it.

When tasked with new assignments that are unlike something she has seen before, her first step is to ask someone else, usually a more senior associate who may have encountered a similar situation, to see if they have existing documentation that could potentially be useful. Then, Etahjayne methodically starts drafting an outline to make the situation more manageable. Even though she may experience impostor syndrome while beginning a new project, she exemplifies the *impostor advantage.*

In this example, Etahjayne follows the *impostor advantage* thought process as she displays emotional intelligence, humility, adaptability, and perseverance. She has the self-awareness to quickly identify what she doesn't know, the humility to reach out to someone else for their input, the adaptability to learn what she needs to do, and the perseverance to get it all done.

* * *

Perseverance is the final characteristic of the *impostor advantage.* An underlying component of the other three characteristics, it is the force which compels someone to display emotional intelligence, humility, and adaptability. Humility, adaptability, and empathy all require a conscious decision to consistently develop and exercise these behaviors. Humility requires the choice to set your own thoughts and opinions aside, to listen to other thought patterns, and to recognize that your successes are the result of a multitude of factors in addition to your own capabilities. Empathy requires the choice to be vulnerable about your own experiences and to share in that vulnerability with someone else. Adaptability requires the choice to put in the effort to adjust to an environment that may originally be outside of your comfort zone. All of these characteristics require hard work and perseverance.

The good thing is that a strong work ethic and sense of determination are not new concepts to the impostor. Someone who has impostor syndrome does not innately enjoy feeling like an impostor. They don't enjoy the stress or anxiety caused by the feeling of not measuring up to their peers or not feeling prepared for an assignment. So, what do they do to work against and compensate for these feelings? They over work themselves. They over-prepare for presentations and work much harder than necessary in order to feel adequately ready for the task at hand. They will do whatever it takes to complete what they have been assigned without revealing any incompetence or weakness to anyone.

Several impostor "types" have been identified as impostor syndrome presents itself in different ways. Though these types have some commonalities, they show the diversity of the impostor phenomenon. Additionally, impostor syndrome is not always clear and may be easily confused with being a perfectionist or workaholic, though these are over-simplifications of impostor syndrome.

The most common archetypes of impostor syndrome include the perfectionist, the superhero, the expert, the natural genius, and the soloist.

The **perfectionist** is never happy with their work and always believes they have room to improve as they fixate on their flaws and mistakes, no matter how small they may be.

The **superhero** drives themselves to work as hard as they possibly can to the point of work addiction because they feel incompetent and working hard is the only way to combat that feeling. If they just keep putting more hours in, they are convinced they will feel more confident.

The **expert** constantly wants to learn more despite their already high level of expertise and never feels comfortable with their own level of understanding. They always want to enrich their knowledge, even if it is beyond what is required.

The **natural genius** sets hard-to-achieve goals for themselves, and then they are vastly disappointed in themselves when they don't meet those goals. Even if they successfully execute on a task, they consider themselves to be a failure if they didn't do it within the timeline they previously defined.

Finally, the **soloist** desires to work by themselves, they pride themselves on their own level of productivity, and they sometimes see asking for help from others as a sign of weakness or incompetence on their part.[30]

---

30   Melody, Wilding, "5 Types of Imposter Syndrome and How to Stop Them," *The Muse*, June 19, 2020.

Each one of these impostor types puts a strong emphasis on working hard to bridge the gap—the gap that the impostor perceives in the knowledge or capabilities they have and the knowledge and capabilities they believe they need to be successful in their respective fields. This is why people with impostor syndrome can struggle with burn out—they push themselves unbelievably hard over and over again. Impostors simply won't settle for not completing something, even if they feel overwhelmed by it. If it's not done, they will stay up until whatever hour to make sure they have gotten their work done at a level that is more than adequate. Impostors paddle as quickly as they need to under the surface in order to present the composed swan on top of the water.

Impostor syndrome runs in my family. Some of the most honest conversations I have had about feeling like an impostor have been with my older sister, Lauren. When we were growing up, Lauren was the bold one, the outspoken one, and the confident one; the one who got dismissed from ballet after the first day for trying to lead the class. I deeply admired her confidence and aspired to find similar confidence of my own one day. Fast forward about twenty years, I don't think anyone was completely surprised when she decided to go to law school. "Badass attorney" fit her aesthetic well. She later joined a niche law firm without any experience in the subject matter. (To be honest, at times I'm still confused about what she does. In the same way that she just knows I make a lot of PowerPoints.) She fully jumped into the challenge of becoming a trusted advisor in a completely new area of law. Lauren works harder than anyone I know—reading case law, attending continuing legal education seminars, and constantly asking questions to partners or other associates. She

CHAPTER 7 · 101

spends a good part of her weekends reviewing case materials and preparing for trials. Her over-preparation is actually how she deals with impostor syndrome. It is how she takes control over the situation. Since only time will determine her level of experience, she can determine her level of preparation. As she has said to me before, "For now, what I lack in experience I make up for in preparation."

Researchers Jaruwan Sakulku and James Alexander further explored the specific methods of working that are associated with the "impostor cycle" first defined by Dr. Clance. In the impostor cycle, an individual feels anxiety when they are assigned a new task, which is followed by a period of over-preparation or procrastination as more than necessary time and effort are put into completing the task or assignment. When the task is successfully completed, a brief period of relief is often quickly followed by a sense of personal failure, because they realized that they were successful due to overpreparation (over-the-top effort) or procrastination (luck) and not because they are more than capable of doing well at their job.

The success or reward of the experience is never fully internalized, and the cycle repeats when the next new task causes a new bout of anxiety and uncertainty. Being their own worst critics, impostors tend to find flaws that other people may not even see and constantly pressure themselves to improve.[31] Impostors demand excellence from themselves as they hold themselves to a higher, if not borderline unreasonable, standard. Sounds miserable, right? Never being happy with yourself or the work that you have done?

31   Jaruwan Sakulku and James Alexander, "The Impostor Phenomenon," *International Journal of Behavior Science* 6, no. 1 (2011): 73-92.

Thriving with Impostor Syndrome in the Digital Age

Well, there is an enormous upside to the perfectionism and unrealistic standards when channeled in a positive direction. Ambition is driven by the desire to achieve more. The dissatisfaction that you may feel with your existing knowledge and capabilities is what makes you crave additional achievements and endeavors. Discontent causes movement and movement is what allows for continuous learning and growing. People who don't get overconfident or complacent about their abilities will continue to propel themselves far into their career.

Impostors are notorious overachievers. They are the type of people who relentlessly push themselves to do more and do better. They are the type of people who make things happen. They don't stop for too long at one juncture before they are ready to go on to the next. Whether they realize it or not, impostors thrive outside of their comfort zone. As impostor syndrome becomes part of their identity, they seek out the opportunities that may appear to be a stretch of their existing qualifications because, even if they don't admit it to themselves, they know they will do what they need to do in order to be and feel qualified. The fear of failure and of being "found out" to be a fraud is what motivates people with impostor syndrome to work even harder. Scientific evidence actually shows that failure is an even stronger motivation than reward, and people actually perform at higher levels when they are concerned about looking incompetent.[32]

The feeling of not wanting to disappoint or be the weakest link makes impostors be better team members who are more than willing to pull their own weight and then some. (This

32 A. J. Elliot, "Approach and avoidance achievement goals: An intrinsic motivation analysis," Unpublished doctoral dissertation, University of Wisconsin-Madison, 1995.

is the exact type of person who you wish was in your group projects in college.) The importance of teamwork and collaboration cannot be overstated in the Digital Age, as it leads to more efficient critical thinking and increased creativity as multiple perspectives are considered when developing solutions to complex problems. Corporations looking to succeed require individuals who are willing to work hard to keep up with the rapid pace of changing systems that shows no chance of slowing down anytime soon. Businesses have and are continuing to adapt to this reality. A McKinsey & Company report on rethinking work in the Digital Age explained that the dynamics of the workplace are shifting to revolve around project-based work versus the definition of specific roles or occupations. Though this type of model is commonly associated with IT development, an increasingly digitalized world means that this method of staffing and working will continue to extend to new industries as they adopt new technologies to remain competitive and efficient. The expectation that employees will more or less fill the same role throughout the duration of their employment is no longer completely true or realistic.[33]

People will have to shift quickly to address whatever the next project holds and be determined to adapt. This new way of staffing has resulted in less emphasis on formal education, licenses, and certifications, and more emphasis on soft skills that can be applied across more than one domain. This all makes sense, since soft skills are more difficult to learn than technical knowledge that can be taught on the job. The consistent "fish out of water" environment tests the ability to adjust and exhibit patience during change.

---

33   Jacques Bughin et al., "Rethinking Work in the Digital Age," *McKinsey Quarterly*, October 24, 2016.

Modern technology has caused us to become impatient. Think about the last time you groaned when your phone or laptop took a couple of extra seconds to load a webpage or sighed because your Amazon Prime package was delayed. We are so accustomed to information being available at our fingertips and getting what we want in a short amount of time. Technology has also made us more impatient toward success. Sensationalized stories of success across the internet seem to perpetuate the myth that we can achieve it practically "overnight." Take the story of Instagram—an app designed for users to share pictures was downloaded over a million times in a matter of months after it launched and was acquired two years later by Facebook for one billion dollars. The main focus of the narrative was on the explosive growth of an app created by two grad students and the major financial reward they received when their innovative idea became the target of a technology titan. There doesn't tend to be as much focus on the less glamorous elements of the process that require perseverance—the countless hours spent developing the app, the search for the right investors, and the continued decision to keep moving forward despite hitting roadblocks. Outside of the example of tech start-ups, the way in which we are able to view snapshots of other people's success stories across LinkedIn again shows the end result and not the process of persistence, which can cause us to question why we have not achieved more ourselves in a short timeframe. Getting impatient with our own progression is relatively easy. Perseverance requires patience—not only patience with ourselves as we continue to grow our own capabilities, but also patience when finding the most optimal solutions to complex problems. Humility is important to realize that sometimes the solutions we think up may not be the best solutions for the problem, while patience is important to realize that the best, most thought-out solutions take time and effort to develop.

It is inevitable that new technology and new processes will present new challenges that require innovative problem solvers who have the perseverance to find a solution because they have previously experienced situations where they have been challenged and had to learn on their feet. Though, challenges at work in the Digital Age are not always technology-related, as we have witnessed throughout the length of 2020. Though working from home was once seen as a coveted perk and a privilege usually reserved for Fridays, prolonged work from home set-ups are now becoming the new normal for many people in the workforce due to required social distancing meant to slow down the spread of a global pandemic. Since companies have learned how to adapt and excel at working remotely by this point (probably because they simply had no choice but to do so), many firms are considering moving to a total or partial remote working model even after the pandemic has passed, as they have decided to offload unnecessary office space and equipment and instead invest in telecommuting collaboration technology.

Constantly working remotely from your home office or even your kitchen table can cause feelings of insecurity to surface that bring about or fuel existing impostor syndrome. Etah-jayne shared with me:

> *Last month we had our annual review, and before we had our face-to-face meeting they sent around an electronic copy that included what everyone who reviewed you had said about you. At first I couldn't open the file. I was certain the feedback would be bad—it was actually glowing. Why did I work myself up into the*

anxious state and have this idea in my head that I wasn't doing a good job when that wasn't the case at all? I think it mostly comes down working from home and not seeing anyone or receiving the face-to-face feedback in real time each day.

One aspect of impostor syndrome is anxiety about appearing smart and wanting to impress your superiors. When you are not face-to-face every day, it becomes more difficult to know if you are in fact measuring up to the standards of management. Because it can be difficult to discern the tones of emails, a single message could cause you to worry whether you are disliked by your boss and make you feel incompetent. Even the fact of not being in an office surrounded by colleagues and a work environment can alter your mindset and make you feel like you are "faking it" even more. Dialing into Teams or Zoom calls with your video off doesn't really make you feel any more qualified in your role or in your own capabilities. Being alone for the greater part of a day makes the inner conversation on self-doubt seem louder. With more distractions at home and a giant blur between work-life balance, days with little productivity can make you feel unmotivated and disheartened. As people work from home for the foreseeable future, the inner critic will continue to surface. However, impostors already have a strong work ethic that is supported by the determination to succeed, and they are already accustomed to the long hours that have now become all too common while working remotely. The next section will explore why that inner conversation of self-doubt is actually a good conversation to have.

As you can see, perseverance is the greatest asset of the impostor because it supports everything the impostor is able to achieve. It allows the impostor to be self-aware, empathetic, willing to learn, and humble about their own accomplishments, because they understand that success is not something you receive but rather something that you have to work at continually. Despite feeling unsure and having overwhelming self-doubts at times, the impostor works hard to not only execute but also to excel in their field. They push through their insecurities to achieve. They are highly motivated to work hard from the fear of showing incompetence, and in doing so they validate they are not incompetent at all. They are driven to push themselves to achieve more than they even originally imagined for themselves and to think critically to solve complex problems.

Though impostor syndrome may outwardly seem like an affliction, a hindrance, or a negative way of thinking, the personal characteristics embedded within the impostor phenomenon are actually crucial to workplace success in the Digital Age. They are the exact types of skills that machines or artificial intelligence will never replace. Impostors are the kinds of people who companies want to hire as they advance their technologies. We are at a time where the tenets of impostor syndrome have become invaluable assets to individuals working in the Digital Age. It is no longer a syndrome, but an advantage to success. The *impostor advantage* allows an individual to tap into their developed and practiced ability to learn and adapt in new situations and environments, to understand their own strengths and weaknesses, and to be a better team player, manager, and friend. The final section will explore the benefits of embracing impostor syndrome and how to develop the *impostor advantage* in your own life.

PART III

Leveraging the
Impostor Advantage

CHAPTER 8

Don't Face It, Embrace It:

Reframing the Dialogue on Impostor Syndrome

———

If you do a quick Google search of impostor syndrome, you will get a series of articles with titles that look something like the following:

"Impostor syndrome: Symptoms and how to deal with it."

"Five steps to overcoming impostor syndrome in the workplace."

"What is impostor syndrome, and how can you combat it?"

The online discourse surrounding impostor syndrome mainly discusses methods of overcoming, combatting, and dealing with any feelings of being "unqualified." Essentially, these types of articles encourage the suppression of that inner questioning voice in your head. They continue the rhetoric that having impostor syndrome is a disadvantage and certainly not something you would want to reveal to someone else. Additionally, these articles perpetuate the idea of impostor syndrome as an individual or personal problem to be corrected or fixed with little consideration for the types of environments that may cause impostor syndrome.

The lack of positive discourse on impostor syndrome was actually a main motivation for me to write this book—to start a vastly different type of discussion on the topic.

The best way to "deal" with impostor syndrome is by embracing it and encouraging others to feel comfortable enough to do the same. It's time to remove the stigma around showing our "humanness" or imperfections at work and understand the power that can be created in an environment where people no longer fear failure.

"We need more leaders to carry the torch of vulnerability and to create a culture of empowerment around feeling vulnerable."

—*MARIO LANZAROTTI*

* * *

Mario Lanzarotti has made it his life's purpose to help people "get unstuck" through his work as a business and mindset coach. This purpose drove him to leave behind growing business partnerships in the New York City fashion industry to create the coaching and speaking company The Power in You, which reaches clients across the globe looking to pivot their lives. I contacted Mario to learn more about how he helps clients who experience impostor syndrome as they undergo changes in their career and life paths.

Mario has leveraged his own impostor syndrome experiences in the process of starting a business from scratch to help other people navigate similar experiences. The guidance Mario gives to his clients does not include shutting down impostor syndrome thoughts of "Am I good enough?" or "Do I really deserve this opportunity?" Instead, he encourages that this inner voice is handled with appreciation and acceptance. When someone starts questioning their own capabilities as they take the next step in their career, it may seem natural to quickly respond to those types of thoughts in a negative way by wanting to "shut up" this inner voice or thinking, *When will I finally get over myself?* Mario discussed how not giving yourself permission to truly feel these impostor feelings and viewing these thought patterns as something that is wrong with you is going into resistance against yourself.

He said, "Every limiting pattern is the belief that somehow you're not good enough—that you're broken or there's something wrong with you; that you need to get your shit together. If you are resisting any part of your human experience, then you are resisting yourself."

I found myself constantly thinking, *Wow, I need to get my shit together*, whenever self-doubt thoughts popped up in my brain. I thought there was something wrong with me or there was something I was lacking and that was why I had these feelings in the first place. If I was *just* smarter or if I *just* had more experience, then I would not feel so unqualified or underprepared. I very much believed I had to do something in order to get rid of these feelings. If you are like me, the term "impostor syndrome" may be a fairly new term for you, or you only recently discovered what having impostor syndrome actually means. You may have been experiencing it long before you heard or fully understood the term, but you weren't sure what to label these kinds of thoughts besides simply "self-doubt" or "insecurity." When I first found out there was a term for what I was experiencing and it was labeled as a "syndrome," I felt more compelled to correct myself. However, Mario pointed out to me that when someone rejects their own impostor thoughts because they think they *shouldn't* feel that way, they end up causing even more discomfort for themselves. Being ashamed or feeling guilty about having impostor thoughts is counterproductive.

I began to think about this concept in terms of a more "concrete" experience. Picture that you are walking along and hit a patch of ice on the street. You lose your footing, and your hands brace your fall to the cold ground. You first look around to see if someone saw, and you bruised your ego in addition to your back. Then the twinges of pain start. Unfortunately, your hands got scraped up when you hit the pavement and your ankle feels sore. You may also feel a little shaken up from the fall. Do you think to yourself, *Wow I shouldn't be in pain or shaken up right now*? Probably not. You realize the context of the situation—you have just slipped on a sheet of ice and gotten a little bruised up in the process. You most likely don't question or deny these feelings you are experiencing. You don't think there is something wrong with you. You accept your reaction to the situation as normal given the circumstances.

So why don't we treat our experiences with impostor syndrome in the same way? Why don't we look at the situation we are in, such as the demanding job propelling us out of our comfort zone, and say, "It's okay for me to feel this way"? Why can't we accept impostor syndrome as a "normal" reaction to situations in which we have great responsibility and high visibility? In a corporate setting, I think we may be too quick to try to place the blame on ourselves or rationalize what is wrong with us personally instead of understanding the context of our experiences. Maybe because it is easier to say, "I'm not qualified for this job" and "I need to figure out how to not feel this way." Taking the one-thousand-foot view of the situation and assessing *why* you feel like an impostor and why that's a perfectly acceptable reaction to your surrounding environment is a more difficult exercise. Why? Because as an "impostor," you believe there is always something more that you could be doing to be better.

Think about a time when you experienced impostor syndrome, and picture yourself back in that moment. Then consider how you would respond to the following questions:

- How would you describe the environment you were in? Was it high stress, fast paced, or rapidly changing?

- Did you feel somewhat "different" than the majority of people who surrounded you (e.g., age, gender, race)?

- Were you engaging in an activity or task that you had never done before?

- Were you doing something you considered outside of your "comfort zone"?

These types of questions help to identify *why* someone may feel undeserving or unqualified instead of focusing on *what* they need to address. This shifts the question from "How do I overcome my impostor syndrome?" to "Why am I experiencing impostor syndrome in the first place?"

It's about reframing the questions we ask ourselves. Language is so important when it comes to discussing impostor syndrome. While the common discourse uses "overcom-ing," "combatting" and "dealing with," it should include more words like "accepting," "allowing," and "embracing." Accepting impostor syndrome as a normal reaction and a common occurrence in a career journey is about accepting vulnerability—the vulnerability that is so important to create a workplace culture of empowerment where people can feel comfortable being their authentic selves and are not intim-idated by the fear of failure.

Going back to the statistic earlier in this book, the majority of people (more than 70 percent) will experience impostor syndrome at least once in their lifetime.[34] Impostor syndrome is a part of the human experience. Why? Because we continue to put ourselves out there by applying for exciting new jobs and trying new activities. Putting yourself out there is never as easy as it looks and requires a commitment to being vul-nerable. If you have experienced impostor syndrome already in some shape or form, there's a good chance you will experi-ence it again, because it shows you are up to the challenge to push yourself to a place where real growth can happen (even if you haven't fully admitted that to yourself yet). You wouldn't feel like an impostor or a fraud if you were doing something that was *easy* or something that comes more naturally to you. Feeling like an impostor is indicative that you are pushing and challenging yourself to do something outside of your comfort zone, and that is an amazing thing.

Somewhere sitting on a back shelf in a HomeGoods store there is a six-by-six white canvas with an inspirational quote in bold, black lettering that says something like, "Life begins at the end of your comfort zone." I usually walk right

---

34   Jaruwan Sakulku and James Alexander, "The Impostor Phenomenon," *International Journal of Behavior Science* 6, no. 1 (2011): 73-92.

past these cheesy workspace additions, but "cheesy" does not mean that the sentiment is untrue. In fact, myself and my fellow "impostors" out there might benefit from having this canvas sitting next to the laptop that we spend a lot of quality time with every day. It's a reminder that feeling in over your head, overwhelmed, and out of your comfort zone is not a negative. Yes, it may seem "uncomfortable" in the moment, but the overall experience is valuable for personal progress. Learning to operate outside of your comfort zone is a crucial skill in a world that offers so many opportunities and is constantly changing. If we didn't take the risks to try things we may feel somewhat unqualified or unprepared for, we would remain stagnant or complacent and not have the chance to see what we are capable of achieving. That is the double-edged nature of impostor syndrome—it is both the consequence and the creator of personal growth. Someone experiencing impostor syndrome is successful, but they attribute that success to something other than their own capabilities. The underplaying of personal abilities and the recognition of continued room for growth is what lays the groundwork for continued success.

The articles out there on the internet describe impostor syndrome from the *consequence* of success perspective and not so much the perspective of *driving* success. The second type of perspective requires dialogue that inner questioning is normal, insecurity is normal, and impostor syndrome is expected during phases of personal and professional growth that lead to success. The challenge is finding, or more so creating, an environment where sharing the thoughts of your inner questioning voice and being vulnerable is supported. As a society we have become so accustomed to sharing details of our lives with many people at one time across social media platforms, but yet it still is uncomfortable sharing details that make us seem less than perfect and put together. Admitting to myself and others that I'm a work-in-progress just trying my best reduced my embarrassment of feeling like a fraud and made me embrace my impostor syndrome even more. I have learned to be unashamed and unapologetic about not knowing something and being unsure of myself. This is simply part of being human and something that has become even more likely due to the rapid pace in which things change and the fact that new information constantly emerges. Admitting to other people that you feel like an "impostor" is not bizarre. Chances are they might have felt that way at some point too in some aspect of their lives, and they might even be able to provide some insight on how they have handled it. I've actually found it quite helpful (and relieving) to discuss my own experiences with other people. Revealing my true feelings of being unsure about my own capabilities and qualifications helped me to feel more authentic and like I wasn't hiding some part of me from other people. I think there is some comfort in knowing you are not the only swan on the water and there are other people out there thinking similar thoughts and having similar feelings as they navigate similar challenges. What is the difference between *dealing* with impostor syndrome versus *embracing* impostor syndrome?

To me, it looks like:

Dealing with impostor syndrome	Embracing impostor syndrome
• *"I shouldn't be feeling this way or questioning myself"*— Ignoring or suppressing thoughts of being unqualified or unprepared.	• *"I am allowed to feel this way, and questioning myself is normal"*— Listening to my own voice and inner critic without judgement.
• *"The way I am thinking is not productive, but I can fix it"*— Viewing impostor thoughts as an irrational response or a personal problem that can be corrected over time with the proper response.	• *"The way I am thinking is not off-base given the current situation"*— Viewing impostor thoughts as a normal reaction to surroundings instead of a personal problem.
• *"I wouldn't feel unqualified if I just learned to change my thought patterns and identify my triggers"*— Focusing on the personal factors contributing to impostor syndrome and not the contextual causes.	• *"I am most likely having these thoughts because this situation is new to me and I'm not sure where I should ask for help"*— Analyzing first *why* impostor syndrome thoughts are occurring instead of *how* to fix it.

- *"I am capable of handling my impostor syndrome on my own"*— Hiding true thoughts from others due to shame or fear of appearing unqualified or unintelligent.

- *"I will share my impostor syndrome thoughts and experiences with others as I continue to navigate my own challenges"*— Embracing vulnerability, sharing experiences with others, and being as authentic as possible.

- *"I have finished my own battle with impostor syndrome, so I don't need to share this experience with others"*— Limiting vulnerability in order to not show any weakness or lack of confidence to others.

- *"If I am vulnerable with others, they may not feel alone in their own impostor syndrome experiences"*— Fostering an environment where others can be comfortable being their authentic selves.

Embracing impostor syndrome leads to the *impostor advantage* by being open to what can be learned from feeling uncomfortable and through having vulnerability around that uncomfortableness. The *impostor advantage* doesn't look at impostor syndrome as a hindrance to personal progress and instead accepts it as a key indicator of future success.

The next chapter will explore additional activities to create your own *impostor advantage*. It's an interactive process of deconstructing concepts, such as personal identity, qualifications, and achievements. This process will reveal that what we think is inauthentic about ourselves is actually genuine, and what we think we are lacking is actually not what is holding us back at all. Are you ready?

CHAPTER 9

The Impostor Advantage Framework:

Your Personal Gap Analysis

———

Business consultants like using frameworks—methods or templates that organize information in order to effectively analyze situations and develop solutions. Often these frameworks consist of some sort of gap analysis, an assessment between the current state and the target state of the business to identify potential areas of focus. Naturally my consultant brain wanted to design a framework for the *impostor advantage*, a way to evaluate "impostor" thoughts and identify how to leverage those thoughts into positive personal growth.

In the last chapter, I asked you to think about the external context of your impostor syndrome experiences and consider the type of environment you operate in, the types of people surrounding you, and whether you were engaging in something outside your comfort zone. In this chapter,

I encourage you to focus more on the internal context to understand how impostor syndrome, when fully embraced, can be a powerful catalyst for personal development.

The *Impostor Advantage Framework* is a personal gap analysis with the following steps:

- **Step #1:** Identify your current state—who are you, and where are you now?

- **Step #2:** Identify your future state—where do you want to be?

- **Step #3:** Identify your gaps—where do you need to improve?

- **Step #4:** Identify your plan to close the gaps—how are you going to get there?

I will explain how I have defined each of these steps and the self-reflection activities I have used in my own life to answer the above questions. If you are up for it, you can complete these activities for yourself too.

STEP #1: IDENTIFY YOUR CURRENT STATE

My personal current state analysis began by asking myself three (somewhat difficult) questions:

- What is my personal identity?

- What skills do I have; what do I know?

- What have I already achieved?

Find a pen and the nearest piece of paper—a notebook, the back of a receipt, an envelope from your most recent bank statement, or even the margin of this book. Got it? Awesome. (I promised this would be an interactive process.)

WHAT IS YOUR PERSONAL IDENTITY?

Write down the three to five components you feel are absolutely central to your personal identity. These are the main elements of who you are—your personality, your beliefs, your priorities, your interests, and your values. On your identity list, put a circle around any components that are recent. In other words, if you would have been asked to create this same list five or ten years ago, what would probably have not been included on it yet? The first step in deconstructing impostor syndrome and leveraging the *impostor advantage* is identifying and recognizing who you are. Sometimes we are too busy trying to figure out what is the next step, who we want to be, and what kind of life we want to live that we don't think a lot about who we really are in the present and everything that has gotten us to this exact point. Self-awareness is the foundation for understanding how you can create your *own* advantage.

Your personal identity includes elements that have remained constant over time and elements that have been added as you go through various stages of life. The person you were even just a couple of years ago may look vastly different from the person you see in the mirror today. Just out of curiosity—did you include your work or job title in your identity list? It is more than fine if you did. Your career is how you spend forty-plus hours of every week, so it definitely takes up a large part of your time and your life. However, this list will show you everything you are about besides your job—your family, your religion, your hobbies, and everything else that makes you the unique person you are. That may seem like an obvious observation, but it may be easy to forget when you are consumed by stress at work because you don't feel qualified or confident in your own abilities. Your job is only one aspect of your entire life.

I wish I could quote the person who developed the phrase, "Your job is what you do, not who you are." This single saying has helped me personally in embracing my impostor syndrome at work. At the end of the day, you have to answer the question, What is the most important to you? Doing everything perfectly at work, or being proud of the person who you are and the personal qualities that you have? I have learned to accept that feeling like an "impostor" is not something that is wrong with me—it's simply the way I react to and approach situations where I feel outside of my comfort zone. In several ways my impostor syndrome has molded me into the type of person that I am. It is what drives me to work harder, to continually learn, and to have understanding for other people who may be feeling the same way.

WHAT SKILLS DO YOU HAVE; WHAT DO YOU ALREADY KNOW?

Take a moment to think about your strengths.

What do you bring to the table in your current job? Do you have superior PowerPoint or Excel skills? Are you good at communicating your ideas to others in a meeting? Do you pay attention to details that others may skip over? What topic could you confidently present on to a room full of people?

Write three to four of these personal strengths down. If you need some help making this list, don't be shy about approaching a colleague you feel comfortable asking. It's important to acknowledge your strengths and the areas where you have confidence. Recognizing what you do know is just as important as recognizing what you don't know (which you will do in Step #3).

WHAT HAVE YOU ACHIEVED ALREADY?

When I sent out a survey last year on topics related to impostor syndrome and social media, the final question I asked survey takers to respond to was, "What are the three achievements you are most proud of in your life?" The majority of responses included similar types of achievements: graduating from college, completing a post-grad program, landing a dream job, or getting a significant promotion. Answers were centered around professional or academic achievements, and few people responded with any other type of achievement. It makes sense—when someone asks us about our top achievements, we go straight into interview mode and highlight resumé accomplishments that showcase our past success in school and in the workplace. As personal identities are made up of more than just where you go to school or what you do for work, achievements can happen in other areas of life.

First, what is an "achievement" anyway? The dictionary definition of "achievement" is simply "a thing done successfully, typically by effort, courage, or skill."[35] With such a broad, generalized definition, achievements in early adulthood can probably be classified into several different types. Academic and professional achievements are the highlights found on your resumé or CV. These types of achievements say you were recognized for excelling in your respective academic or professional field by receiving a scholarship, appearing on

---

35 *Oxford English Dictionary*, (Oxford: Oxford University Press, 2020), s.v. "Achievement."

the dean's list, or being named as the top sales performer in the office. However, not all achievements come in the form of certificates, diplomas, plaques, and shiny medals that sit on your desk. Sometimes we forget the importance of our *personal* achievements. I'm talking about the stuff we accomplish that doesn't get its own line on a resumé or a framed award—the types of accomplishments we don't think to bring up during interviews when a hiring manager asks, "So, what is your greatest achievement to date?" In fact, we may not share these "accomplishments" with anyone at all. By personal achievements, I don't mean creative hobbies, successful relationships, and starting families, though those are all important. What I am referring to is the accomplishment of handling difficult situations and challenges thrown at you over the course of your life. It was when you overcame any underlying factors or personal circumstances that could have hindered you from succeeding in your professional or academic life. I like to refer to these as the "despite" or "even though" achievements. As in "Even though __, I was able to __." and "Despite __, I __." Perhaps our own stories of triumph in adversity, of perseverance and resilience, may be some of our most important achievements to date.

Now write down your top five achievements that you would feel comfortable sharing on a resumé, a LinkedIn page, or during an interview with a hiring manager for your dream job. Below that list that you have just created write down five personal achievements, the exciting things you have shared with friends and family, and the types of achievements you have kept to yourself (or maybe didn't even think of as achievements until now). Yes, it may seem a bit awkward to do this exercise. It may even seem a little challenging to pinpoint your greatest life achievements. When we are in the moment of taking steps, or making achievements, toward the peak of the mountain we are climbing, it is easy to lose sight of everything below while we are looking closely at the top. These are the elements of our personal history, where we came from, and everything we have done to get to this exact point in our lives. I will be honest that when I pulled out my resumé for the first time in a while when deciding to apply for new jobs, I was a little caught off guard. I had forgotten about some of the experiences and what I had accomplished in roles that I had prior to 2017.

Our achievements are what we typically use to determine and validate our qualifications. We reference academic and professional accomplishments to figure out if we are "qualified" for a particular job. If an open position lists that candidates are required to have four-plus years of experience and additional certifications, we compare against our own achievements to determine if we are fit for the role. We don't tend to think about qualifications we may have that are not clearly stated on our resumés. Maybe this is part of the problem. If we solely focus on aligning our previous work experience to the job description, we will likely feel unprepared every time we start a new role. It is important to distinguish between *being* qualified and *feeling* qualified. By *being* qualified, I mean aligning academic and professional achievements. And by *feeling* qualified, I mean aligning personal qualifications— what you have achieved despite, although, and even though. This allows you to start feeling more deserving and prepared your current situation.

Feeling qualified is becoming more important than being qualified in the Digital Age. With rapidly evolving technology and innovation, it is unlikely you will know absolutely everything you encounter in an office setting. At some point you will have to adapt and learn something new. *Feeling* qualified provides the confidence to adapt and creates some sense of deserving new accomplishments that come your way. If you allow yourself to feel qualified for a particular opportunity because you recognize all that you have managed to push through and overcome to get that exact point, you will be more capable of internalizing the success.

While identifying your own achievements, it's important to understand that not everyone's list will look the same as yours. A phrase I have heard quite often recently is "measure with your own yardstick," which is helpful to think about if you start to fall down the rabbit hole of feeling upset that your own achievements don't seem like enough in comparison. Not everyone is going to be a CEO of a startup by thirty, and that's okay. When we engage in comparing our own list of achievements to other people's achievements on public display, we are forgetting to look at the whole picture. Not every accomplishment is posted online in a status update or Instagram post.

What do we do with the personal accomplishments that maybe are not so happy or are *too* personal to share with our friends and followers online? Virtually, nothing. Even though the "even though" achievements we have will never be memorialized on Facebook or Twitter or used as a caption on an Instagram post, they are a large part of our individual stories and identities. Our online persona, the fragmented glimpses of our identity that exist across various social media sites, is incomplete and does not encompass all aspects of our achievements. Social media is quite literally filtered snapshots of our lives and not a continuously rolling film of everything that happens. Instead of being a mirror reflection of our lives and every little thing we do, we can see social media sites as platforms for personal branding. In personal branding, it's only natural to want to show off your best achievements, qualities, attributes, and experiences. The world doesn't have to see all of your achievements for them to be real; however, it's important for you to see them.

By fully recognizing all types of our achievements, we are able to start to acknowledge all of the steps that were needed to reach the top of the mountain and that our personal achievements are just as meaningful and important as other kinds of achievements. Taking the time to reflect and make an achievement list prior to or after starting something new—a new job or academic program—provides a necessary "grounding," if you will. You don't have to make this list on your own either. Engaging those who are closest to you can help you recognize accomplishments you may have completely forgotten or glossed over, especially personal accomplishments. On the flip side, you can help other people develop their own achievement lists when they are feeling uncertain by recognizing times when you witnessed them push through a challenging situation or persevere in an inspiring way.

Impostor syndrome is rooted in a type of forgetfulness. A key aspect of impostorism is not being able to internalize success. In other words, it is the failure to acknowledge exactly what we *have* accomplished already while keeping in mind that there is more than just one type of achievement and everyone will have their own unique list of achievements. By making this kind of effort to identify all types of achievements we start to feel more deserving of our own success and are less likely to attribute our future achievements to luck or good timing. Rather, we start to see them as logical next steps and meaningful progress. We can genuinely start to feel proud of ourselves as we see the tremendous growth we have had even just over a few years. When you start questioning if and when you will get to the next step, take a moment to pause and appreciate all of the steps you have already taken because there is a good chance you might have forgotten a few.

STEP #2: IDENTIFY YOUR FUTURE STATE

You've completed what is probably the most difficult part of the framework for impostors by identifying where you are at and what you have done to get there. Now to a relatively easier step for impostors: identifying your future state. Where do you want to be?

After you feel you have a solid understanding of where you are now and your personal current state, you can begin to determine your desired future state. What is your ideal or end goal? Is it confidence in your current role or the confidence to apply for a new job with more responsibility? Is it feeling more comfortable expressing your own ideas? Is it learning a new skillset or the development of an existing skillset? Or is it trying something completely outside of your comfort zone?

Keeping in mind your current standing, think about where you would like to be that you could achieve in a reasonable timeline. List a few goals you have for the next one to five years, no matter how large or small they are.

STEP #3: IDENTIFY THE GAPS

Impostor syndrome provides a type of self-awareness that allows you to be hyper aware of what you are "lacking"—the knowledge or skills that you feel you must learn to keep up in your work environment. Once you have recognized what you *do* know and where you want to go, you can assess what you need to learn without feeling like you are inadequate. What do you want to improve in order to achieve your goals?

If you are an "impostor," the next list may be a lot easier for you to draft than the one you created for your lists of strengths and existing skills.

After you analyze where you want to be, it's time to think about what you believe is holding you back. Take a moment to think about what you don't know. What could you be better at? What topic would you feel uncomfortable presenting on in a room full of people? What skills do you feel you could learn to be more effective at your job? What makes you feel "behind" in comparison to your peers or colleagues? What do you feel you need to learn in order to obtain your "dream" job? Is there a particular subject or area of expertise you feel like you have limited knowledge of?

Consider these questions and write down three to four of these improvement areas, and be as descriptive as you possibly can, clearly outlining why you feel like you have a knowledge "gap" in these areas.

STEP #4: IDENTIFY YOUR PLAN TO CLOSE THE GAPS

Lastly, how are you going to get there? Now instead of thinking about the above points as knowledge "gaps," think of these as knowledge progression points. Circle the one you could reasonably achieve in the next six months to a year. This is your next step. When you start to question your own qualifications and your preparedness for the situation you are currently in, leverage your "impostor" self-awareness to identify the skills you are already equipped with and to select the skills you would like to improve. This gives actionable items to work toward instead of being overwhelmed by everything that you feel you "don't know."

Harnessing the *impostor advantage* and its emphasis on the ability to develop and enhance your own personal talent and skills is critical for thriving professionally in the Digital Age. By clearly acknowledging what you do know, what you sort of know, and what you don't know, the narrative shifts from feeling like you don't know anything to understanding the progression of knowledge. Admitting you don't know something can be an uncomfortable feeling. No one feels great about telling someone else they feel like they are struggling to keep up or to grasp concepts, especially when you feel like there are set expectations to reach a certain knowledge level. In this case, perspective is absolutely everything. Instead of looking at the need to learn as a sign of some deficit in your current knowledge, learning can be seen as an enhancement in your current knowledge base. Embracing this growth mindset provides more agency over what you can do and what you can achieve if you are willing to invest the time.

Implementing the next step you have identified is not just about choosing what you are going do but also how you are going to approach it. Impostor syndrome is grounded in personal mindset and perception. It is a mindset that prevents us from fully accepting and internalizing our own achievements and successes based on the perception that these achievements and successes are not ours to claim. As impostor syndrome is a mindset, the *impostor advantage* is also a mindset. It is accepting what you know and what you have achieved so far, as well as acknowledging that you will never stop growing and learning because you will never know everything.

The *impostor advantage* is not a complete dismissal of impostor syndrome but rather a redirection of thought and a revision of the long-term view. You can accept the fact that you may be "faking it 'til you make it" in some aspect of your life while also understanding that you are in the continual process of learning. Creating the *impostor advantage* requires embracing and accepting your impostor syndrome thoughts, then shifting those thoughts into meaningful next steps for your own personal growth.

On the following pages are some examples of how I reframed my own impostor thoughts into affirmations for each of the elements of the *impostor advantage*.

Impostor Syndrome	*Impostor Advantage*
• "I feel like I don't know anything."	• "I accept that there are many things I do know, many things I don't know, and many things I will learn."
• "Everyone here is smarter or more capable than I am, so I don't belong here."	• "I may be surrounded by people who seem like they know more than I do, but I have my own strengths to share and this is also an opportunity to learn from others."
• "I only got this job because the hiring manager was feeling generous, I suppose."	• "I realize success is not just a solo journey and my accomplishments are the result of multiple factors, including my own capabilities and talents."

ADAPTABILITY

Impostor Syndrome	Impostor Advantage
• "I feel like I am in way over my head and completely outside of my comfort zone."	• "Though it may be difficult at first, operating outside of my comfort zone will give me the chance to expand my capabilities and develop a new skillset."
• "I feel like I don't have enough existing knowledge to be successful in this role."	• "My capacity and willingness to learn is more important than any knowledge gaps that I have."
• "I am worried people will think I am not smart enough to handle this."	• "Though other people may not see it, I am continuously learning and improving myself while trying my best."

EMOTIONAL INTELLIGENCE/EMPATHY

Impostor Syndrome	Impostor Advantage
• "If I reveal I am unsure of myself, my peers or coworkers will think I am weak or not capable."	• "Showing my vulnerability is a strength and not a weakness—it's important to be in an environment where I feel comfortable being vulnerable and that I have a team that will support me."
• "I feel like I am struggling under the surface, and no one knows or understands that."	• "My experiences and struggles are helping me evolve into the type of leader who is compassionate and understanding toward others."
• "I feel ashamed of myself when I make mistakes because I feel like I am letting others down."	• "I will show myself the same compassion that I would show others in this situation. I understand that everyone, including myself, is just doing the best that they can."

PERSEVERANCE

Impostor Syndrome	*Impostor Advantage*
• "If I just work harder then I won't feel like an impostor or fraud anymore and will be confident in my own capabilities."	• "I am not there yet, but I can get there. I am determined to continue to work hard and put my best effort forward, but I acknowledge that some days I still may feel unsure of myself."
• "Though I've been lucky in the past and working extra hard at the final stage has paid off, this may be the time I actually fail and disappoint people."	• "Though it's difficult to know exactly how things will turn out, I know I have it in me to figure this out, because I will work hard to make it happen."

These statements have helped me accept impostor syndrome as part of my experience and to recognize the positive lessons I have learned from feeling like a "fraud."

If you might be experiencing impostor syndrome, you can create your own *impostor advantage* affirmations or scripts in your own voice or language by using the following process:

Step #1: Take a distinct thought you have had related to your own impostor syndrome experience—a thought about feeling unqualified or worrying about having your insecurities revealed to others at work or at school.

Step #2: Determine how you can use that thought to propel your own personal progress by identifying the positive takeaways of the situation. For example, "I may feel __, but I recognize that this is an opportunity to __" or "I can __, even though I still may feel unsure of myself."

I have provided some ways I have personally found helpful to reflect on some of the important internal questions for developing the *impostor advantage* by considering personal identity, strengths, and weaknesses. Feel free to save the answers you have written down as a reminder to yourself the next time you feel impostor syndrome thoughts popping up in your head as you take on a new role or a new assignment. I hope this list you created will bring perspective to your own situation and the affirmations will provide you with the confidence needed to embrace your impostor syndrome.

EPILOGUE

From One Impostor to Another

In the beginning of this book, I admitted to you that writing this book gave me a strong case of impostor syndrome. I had experienced impostor syndrome at work numerous times in the beginning of my career, but making the decision to write a book (and complete the entire process) was one of the most challenging experiences of impostorism I have ever faced. Yes, I completely see the irony of writing a book *about* impostor syndrome when you are writing the book *with* impostor syndrome. I felt that many hours spent "working on the book" included me trying to convince myself that I was qualified to write *this* book or even *a* book in the first place. I was trying to convince myself that my own message was worthy of being heard, even though I didn't have a degree in psychology or ten-plus years of work experience. Trying to find an answer to why anyone would want to read my book was not helping me to make any progress. I had started talking myself out of writing because I was too caught up in whether I was "qualified" to be doing what I was doing and how other people would perceive my qualifications. The fear

I had of not being "qualified" and not being capable enough was stopping me from realizing what I actually was capable of doing.

Continuing to navigate my own experiences with impostor syndrome while writing this book provided me with a new perspective. The process of doing something completely out of my comfort zone has taught me so much about impostor syndrome and what thriving with it looks like for me personally outside of what I have read about in self-help pieces and heard from life coaches. So, what exactly did I learn through this experience?

IMPOSTOR SYNDROME IS A SIGN OF GROWTH

Feeling like an impostor is more than okay and it is not a sign of failure. Questioning yourself is normal. In fact, it shows a lot about your own ability to self-evaluate and look inward. Additionally, feeling this way most likely means you are in a situation where you will be able to learn and grow. Feeling like an impostor is indicative of you doing something out of your comfort zone because you wouldn't question your own qualifications or overall preparedness if you were doing something easy. It also shows that you recognize you have room for growth so you feel comfortable and confident in what you are doing. Last year I started to feel stagnant in the types of projects I was doing at work. I had gotten to a place where I felt confident in the tasks I was carrying out every day, but I felt like I was no longer learning or growing. I had the opportunity to leave and go somewhere else where there was a better chance I would be given more responsibility and be more challenged at work. It was definitely taking a risk to consider taking a new job with so much uncertainty during a pandemic. Even after I signed my offer and was preparing for my first day of work, I wondered if I was going to be good at this job and if I was truly qualified or if the team had misjudged my capabilities and what I brought to the table. My impostor syndrome, which had taken a short sabbatical, was back in full force. Yes, it wasn't great to have these types of feelings and insecurities resurface, but it was a sign that I was going to go through a period of professional and personal growth. I was probably going to be challenged and wonder if I was truly prepared for this new role, but at the same time I would have the chance to absorb new information and acquire a new skillset. Feeling like an impostor propels personal growth whether we realize it or not. If your next move scares you just a little bit, you are probably headed in the right direction.

IMPOSTOR SYNDROME IS NOT PREDICTABLE

Impostor syndrome comes in waves—one day you may not feel like an impostor. You might feel confident and capable in what you know and what you are doing, and the impostor monster might take a break. Then the next day you may be in a situation where you are presented with a task or a scenario of uncertainty that causes feelings of fraud or phoniness to creep back in, and you wonder how you even got to such a place when you were this "unqualified." Impostor syndrome may affect one area of your life or multiple areas at once. It may be felt short term or long lasting with months or even years of feeling like an impostor. For example, when you start a new job or new role you may feel initially like an impostor—wondering how you got in that particular role in the first place. This feeling may start to subside as you get more ingrained in the role and feel more confident in your own capabilities to accomplish what is asked of you. However, you could be presented with a task you have never seen before that makes you feel anxious, not knowledgeable, and causes your impostor syndrome to return as you ask yourself, "Do I even know what I'm doing here?"

IMPOSTOR SYNDROME IS SITUATIONAL

I have read articles that say impostor syndrome is a lifelong experience, and I think that statement deserves a bit more context. To me, it almost seems to imply that impostor syndrome is some kind of chronic issue that someone will have to deal with their entire life if they don't ever fully address it. That depiction fails to acknowledge that impostor syndrome is deeply ingrained in personal characteristics. It's not necessarily something people suffer from, but rather it's an indication of the type of person they are, how they perceive themselves, and how they perceive others. Impostor syndrome is very situational, in my opinion. Your experience with it—the severity and duration of feelings of being an impostor—will vary based on the type of situation you are experiencing and will likely end once that situation is over.

IMPOSTOR SYNDROME IS NOT A TABOO TOPIC ANYMORE

The majority of people will experience impostor syndrome at some point in their lives, whether it is in an academic, professional, or personal sense. Admitting to other people that you feel like an impostor is not bizarre, because there is a high probability they may have had similar experiences.

Discussing my own experiences with other people has helped me to feel more authentic. Admitting to myself and to others that I'm very much a work-in-progress was relieving. I have learned to not feel ashamed or embarrassed about not knowing something or for being unsure of myself, especially in a highly demanding work environment. This is simply part of being human and something that will continue to be normal with the constant emergence of new information and technology. It's impossible to know everything, so it's less important how much you know and more important how committed you are to continue learning.

IMPOSTOR SYNDROME IS A PERSONAL EXPERIENCE

Impostor syndrome will look different for everyone—for some people it may be a subtle feeling, and for others it may be more severe than that. While talking with others can be very helpful in feeling more authentic, impostor syndrome is still very much an individual experience, as it is rooted in not being able to internalize your own successes. Your friends and family can listen to you talk about situations in which you feel like an impostor and hear your beliefs that you have gotten to where you are in life based on luck. However, no one can prove to you that you are competent and qualified. You have to do this for yourself. You have to determine for yourself what you do and do not know. You have to determine for yourself what you have already accomplished and what you have yet to accomplish. As I have mentioned, impostor syndrome really is embedded in self-reflection.

IMPOSTOR SYNDROME IMPACTS YOUR PERSPECTIVE AND INTERACTIONS WITH OTHERS

Impostor syndrome has definitely impacted how I perceive and interact with the people around me. It has made me more compassionate and patient with others, especially when I have had the opportunity to be in a management role. I fully understand how nerve-wracking it can be when you feel like you are not prepared for a task you were assigned and how it makes you question your own abilities. I realize how terrifying failure can seem, as it can be a self-indicator that you are unfit for the role you are in, which has made me aspire to be the kind of manager who is supportive of her team—making sure they are comfortable with what they have been assigned but not afraid of making mistakes either. I believe that my impostor syndrome has played a large role in how I relate to other people, as it has also taught me a lot about humility and open-mindedness. As I have acknowledged, there are so many things I do not know; I have been inclined to listen and to learn from other people, especially those who have a different perspective from my own. Recognizing I am surrounded by very capable, intelligent people, I have channeled my fear that I do not know enough in comparison to motivation to want to learn from these people and absorb the knowledge they have to offer.

IMPOSTOR SYNDROME ENCOURAGES GRATITUDE

Impostor syndrome has also impacted how I view and perceive new opportunities. When I accepted a new job offer, that acceptance was met with some anxiety if I could handle the role or if I would actually be in way over my head. Though I was anxious, I felt extremely grateful that I had gotten the opportunity in the first place, even if it was above my perceived skillset. I was grateful that I was given the chance to at least see what I could be capable of in a new job, and this gratitude motivated me to want to work hard and be a strong team member. I can't necessarily say I totally believe in luck. I believe there is a reason why you got to where you are, even if you can't see it yourself. In my opinion, those opportunities where we question if we are in the right place are usually the ones meant to help us grow and shape us as people. Being grateful for what you have in life allows you to find happiness in your own situation, and this happiness provides you with the motivation to positively confront challenges and to pursue your goals and ambitions. That's not to say that having gratitude is easy. It is a conscious thought exercise to list the things that you have gratitude for and to continually remind yourself of the appreciation you have for these things, even on the less-than pleasant days.

IMPOSTOR SYNDROME IS NOT A ROADBLOCK TO SUCCESS

As previously discussed, some of the most successful people have felt like impostors at one point, which may come as a shocking surprise to everyone who has witnessed their success. Though the "impostor" is unable to process, internalize, or comprehend their own successes, they are objectively still successful. The inability to internalize success does not make someone unsuccessful. I have learned that having impostor syndrome does not limit me from being successful, though I may not recognize my own successes at times. In many ways, my impostor syndrome is what has propelled me forward in my career by challenging me to look my insecurities in the face and motivating me to work harder to expand my own capabilities.

Though each person's experience with impostor syndrome is different, I still wanted to share the lessons I have learned through my own encounters with it in hopes that they may resonate with someone else. The situations in which impostor syndrome arises may vary, but there are some commonalities in how impostor syndrome molds a person. In other words, impostors share very similar personal characteristics. I hope these lessons may be helpful to you if you are encountering impostor syndrome in some aspect of your life or make you feel more prepared when these kinds of thoughts visit you in the future. I hope these points will allow you to appreciate the positive aspects of experiencing impostor syndrome and encourage you to keep taking risks, pushing yourself out of your comfort zone, and reminding yourself of everything you have achieved already.

I hope it shows you that you can absolutely thrive with impostor syndrome in the Digital Age.

So keep swimming, swans.

APPENDIX

———

INTRODUCTION

Gravois, John. "You're not fooling anyone." *The Chronicle of Higher Education,* November 9, 2007. https://www.chronicle.com/article/youre-not-fooling-anyo-ne/c_nonce=g3eiln7en-7lq76vfpevnj&cid=reg_wall_signup.

Heitmann, Blair. "Encountering a Quarter-life Crisis? You're Not Alone…" *LinkedIn Online Blog,* November 15, 2017. https://blog.linkedin.com/2017/november/15/encountering-a-quarter-life-crisis-you-are-not-alone.

Sakulku, Jaruwan and James Alexander. "The Impostor Phenomenon." *International Journal of Behavior Science* 6, no. 1 (2011): 73-92. https://www.sciencetheearth.com/uploads/2/4/6/5/24658156/2011_sakulku_the_impostor_phenomenon.pdf.

CHAPTER 1

Clance, Pauline and Suzanne Imes. "The Impostor Phenomenon in High Achieving Women: Dynamics and therapeutic intervention." *Psychotherapy: Theory, Research & Practice* 15, no. 3 (1978): 241–247. https://doi.org/10.1037/h0086006.

Leadem, Rose. "12 Leaders, Entrepreneurs and Celebrities Who Have Struggled With Imposter Syndrome." *Entrepreneur,* November 8, 2017. https://www.entrepreneur.com/slideshow/304273.

Romm, Cari. "Impostor Syndrome Can Be a Self-Fulfilling Prophecy." *The Cut,* November 16, 2016. https://www.thecut. com/2016/11/impostor-syndrome-at-work-can-be-a-self-fulfilling-prophecy.html.

Sakulku, Jaruwan, and James Alexander. "The Impostor Phenomenon." *International Journal of Behavior Science* 6, no. 1 (2011): 73-92. https://www.sciencetheearth.com/ uploads/2/4/6/5/24658156/2011_sakulku_the_impostor_phenomenon.pdf.

CHAPTER 2

American Psychiatic Association. "Americans Say They are More Anxious than a Year Ago; Baby Boomers Report Greatest Increase in Anxiety." May 7, 2018. https://www.psychiatry.org/ newsroom/apa-public-opinion-poll-annual-meeting-2018.

Brigham, Tess. "I've been a 'millennial therapist' for more than 5 years—and this is their No. 1 complaint." *CNBC Make It: Science of Success.* July 2, 2019. https://www.cnbc.com/2019/07/02/a-millennial-therapist-brings-up-the-biggest-complaint-they-bring-up-in-therapy.html.

"The Evolution of Social Media: How Did It Begin and Where Could It Go Next?" Maryville Online, Maryville University.

March 3, 2021. https://online.maryville.edu/blog/evolution-social-media/.

Fitzmaurice, Rosie. "This is the exact age when you're most likely to experience a quarter-life crisis — and how to deal with it if you do." *Insider,* November 5, 2017. https://www.businessinsider.com/how-to-deal-with-a-quarter-life-crisis-2017-11.

Fottrell, Quentin. "People Spend Most of Their Waking Hours Staring at Screens." *MarketWatch,* August 4, 2018. www.marketwatch.com/story/people-are-spending-most-of-their-waking-hours-staring-at-screens-2018-08-01.

Tamir, Diana and Jason Mitchell. "Disclosing Information about the Self Is Intrinsically Rewarding." *PNAS, Proceedings of the National Academy of Sciences.* May 2, 2012. www.pnas.org/content/early/2012/05/01/1202129109.

CHAPTER 4

Duchene, Patricia. "The Evolving Workplace." *Forbes,* March 13, 2019. www.forbes.com/sites/patriciaduchene/2019/03/12/the-evolving-workplace/.

Dweck, Carol. "What Having a "Growth Mindset" Actually Means." *Harvard Business Review,* January 13, 2016. https://hbr.org/2016/01/what-having-a-growth-mindset-actually-means.

O'Brien, Michael. "Are Soft Skills More Important than the Right Qualifications?" *Human Resource Executive,* March 12, 2019. https://hrexecutive.com/are-soft-skills-more-important-than-the-right-qualifications/.

Manyika, James et al., "Harnessing automation for a future that works." *McKinsey Global Institute.* January 12, 2017. https://

www.mckinsey.com/~/media/McKinsey/Featured%20Insights/
Digital%20Disruption/Harnessing%20automation%20for%20
a%20future%20that%20works/MGI-A-future-that-works_Full-
report.pdf.

CHAPTER 5

Bergland, Christopher. "The Neuroscience of Empathy."
Psychology Today, October 10, 2013. www.psychologytoday.com/
us/blog/the-athletes-way/201310/the-neuroscience-empathy.

Brown, Brené. 2010. "The Power of Vulnerability." Filmed June
2010 in Houston, Texas. TED video, 20:03. https://www.ted.com/
talks/brene_brown_the_power_of_vulnerability?language=en.

Capgemini Research Institute, *Emotional Intelligence Research,
Executive Survey*, August–September 2019. https://www.
capgemini.com/wp-content/uploads/2019/10/Infographic-
%E2%80%93-Emotional-intelligence-1.pdf.

Goleman, Daniel and Richard Boyatzis. "Emotional Intelligence
Has 12 Elements. Which Do You Need to Work On?" *Harvard
Business Review*, December 5, 2017. www.hbr.org/2017/02/
emotional-intelligence-has-12-elements-which-do-you-need-to-
work-on.

"How Do Social Media Algorithms Work?" Digital Marketing
Institute. May 3, 2019. https://digitalmarketinginstitute.com/
blog/how-do-social-media-algorithms-work.

Oliveira Silva, Patrícia, Liliana Maia, Joana Coutinho,
Brandon Frank, José Miguel Soares, Adriana Sampaio, and
Óscar Gonçalves. "Empathy by Default: Correlates in the
Brain at Rest." *Psicothema* 30, no. 1 (2018): 97-103. doi: 10.7334/
psicothema2016.366.

CHAPTER 6

Bennett, Terry. "Humility Required for Digital Era Success." *Institute for Digital Transformation.* Accessed June 15, 2018. https://www.institutefordigitaltransformation.org/humility-required-digital-era-success/.

Bergland, Christopher. "The Neuroscience of Empathy." *Psychology Today.* New York: Sussex Publishers, October 10, 2013. www.psychologytoday.com/us/blog/the-athletes-way/201310/the-neuroscience-empathy.

"Dunning-Kruger Effect." *Psychology Today,* Sussex Publishers. www.psychologytoday.com/us/basics/dunning-kruger-effect.

Hess, Edward. "Humility: The No. 1 Job Skill Needed for the Smart Machine Age." *Forbes,* May 18, 2015. https://www.forbes.com/sites/darden/2015/05/18/humility-the-1-job-skill-needed-for-the-smart-machine-age/?sh=2cb957596c06.

Obama, Barack. (speech, campaign event, Roanoke, Virginia, July 13, 2012). https://obamawhitehouse.archives.gov/the-press-office/2012/07/13/remarks-president-campaign-event-roanoke-virginia.

CHAPTER 7

Bughin, Jacques, Susan Lund, Jaana Remes. "Rethinking Work in the Digital Age." *McKinsey Quarterly,* October 24, 2016. https://www.mckinsey.com/business-functions/organization/our-insights/rethinking-work-in-the-digital-age#.

Elliot, A. J. "Approach and avoidance achievement goals: An intrinsic motivation analysis." Unpublished doctoral dissertation, University of Wisconsin-Madison. 1995.

Sakulku, Jaruwan, and James Alexander. "The Impostor Phenomenon." *International Journal of Behavior Science* 6, no. 1 (2011): 73-92. https://www.sciencetheearth.com/uploads/2/4/6/5/24658156/2011_sakulku_the_impostor_phenomenon.pdf.

Wilding, Melody. "5 Types of Imposter Syndrome and How to Stop Them." *The Muse*, June 19, 2020. www.themuse.com/advice/5-different-types-of-imposter-syndrome-and-5-ways-to-battle-each-one.

CHAPTER 8

Sakulku, Jaruwan, and James Alexander. "The Impostor Phenomenon." *International Journal of Behavior Science* 6, no. 1 (2011): 73-92. https://www.sciencetheearth.com/uploads/2/4/6/5/24658156/2011_sakulku_the_impostor_phenomenon.pdf.

CHAPTER 9

Oxford English Dictionary. Oxford: Oxford University Press, 2020. https://www.lexico.com/definition/achievement.

Made in the USA
Middletown, DE
29 June 2021

43108905R00086